OUT OF THE BARRIO

OUT OF THE BARRIO

Toward a New Politics of Hispanic Assimilation

LINDA CHAVEZ

BasicBooks
A Division of HarperCollins*Publishers*

Library of Congress Cataloging-in-Publication Data

Chavez, Linda.
Out of the barrio: toward a new politics of Hispanic assimilation /
Linda Chavez.
  p. cm.
Includes bibliographical references and index.
ISBN 0-465-05430-7
  1. Hispanic Americans—Cultural assimilation. 2. Hispanic
Americans—Politics and government. I. Title.
E184.S75C48 1991   91-70060
305.868—dc20   CIP

In memory of my father,
Rudolph F. Chavez

CONTENTS

ACKNOWLEDGMENTS

Many people and organizations helped make this book possible. It would not have been written without the financial and intellectual support of the Manhattan Institute. William Hammett, president of the Manhattan Institute, saw in my proposal to write a book about Hispanics an opportunity to explore important issues of social policy that will influence the future of the Hispanic population and the nation. Lawrence Mone, vice president for research, gave unstintingly of his time, counsel, and encouragement during the difficult months spent writing this book. In addition to the Manhattan Institute, several foundations contributed funds that enabled me to devote myself to full-time research and writing: the John M. Olin Foundation, the Angeles T. Arredondo Foundation, the Lynde and Harry Bradley Foundation, and the Strake Foundation.

I also thank the individuals who generously nursed this project along by helping me analyze data, by sharing research, and generally holding my novice hand. Peter Skerry allowed me to raid his file cabinets and pick his brains, saving me hours of time and providing valuable insights on issues he has thought and written about for more than a decade. Abigail Thernstrom, whose book *Whose Votes Count? Affirma-*

tive Action and Minority Voting Rights provided much of the seed work for my chapter on Hispanics and the Voting Rights Act, has long influenced my thinking on the civil rights issues discussed in this book. Lawrence Mead, Randall Filer, and June O'Neill generously read drafts of certain chapters and offered suggestions that improved the final product. Nabeel Alsalam and Finis Welch and Associates provided the expertise and technical assistance necessary to analyze unpublished data from Current Population Surveys from 1986 and 1988, which provided the basis for my analysis of earnings and education data on Mexican American and Mexican immigrant men.

Many individuals, some of whom no doubt do not share my views, provided me with information necessary to complete this project. While it is impossible to thank each person who extended help, the following persons were particularly gracious: Carlos Medina, Jorge del Pinal, Rafael Valdivieso, Harry Pachon, Rob Paral, Raul Yzaguirre, Julie Quiroz, Bill Diaz, Alejandro Portes, and Frank Bean.

Without the guidance of Martin Kessler, president and editorial director of Basic Books, this book would have remained a series of loosely tied essays. Martin helped me see how to shape this effort into a book. Few first-time authors are as lucky as I was in having such wisdom to guide me. I would also like to thank David Haproff, project editor at Basic, and Otto Sonntag, copy editor, for their assistance in editing the final manuscript.

Finally, I would like to thank my family, especially my husband, Chris Gersten, who encouraged me in this endeavor as he has throughout my career. He patiently read and reread drafts of the manuscript, offering suggestions that improved the flow of language and ideas. My children—David, Pablo, and Rudy—patiently bore my long hours at the computer. Even my mother chipped in with long distance encouragement. My family's support made the sometimes difficult days bearable with their affection and humor.

INTRODUCTION

"We cannot assimilate—and we won't!" The words reverberate through the hall as the crowd of mostly Mexican American students clap their hands wildly. The man shouting from the podium is Arnold Torres, former executive director of the League of United Latin American Citizens, the oldest Hispanic civil rights organization in the United States. The scene is a familiar one, though the setting is new. Torres and I are debating the future of Hispanics before an audience at Stanford University. The young men and women in the audience wear blue jeans and T-shirts, proclaiming their loyalties to rock groups and social causes with equal enthusiasm. In a few years most of this youthful radicalism will be bridled by mortgage payments on suburban homes. But for now these students want no part of the Anglo establishment.

Torres's words strike me as odd. Surely he can't be talking about these kids, or about himself or me or any one of the other Mexican Americans onstage: a Pulitzer Prize–winning journalist, a tenured professor, and an assistant to the governor of California. In fact, Torres's purpose is not so much to suggest that Hispanics are incapable of entering the mainstream as to exhort them to remain outside—separate and distinct from the majority culture. It is a view widely shared by Hispanic leaders, though rarely expressed so boldly.

Today more than twenty-one million Hispanics are living in the United States, and the Hispanic population is increasing five times as fast as the rest of the population. Some demographers predict that in less than a hundred years Hispanics will account for nearly one-third of the nation's people. If Torres's view prevails, and Hispanics either cannot or will not assimilate, it will represent a dramatic shift in the history of American ethnic groups and could alter the fate of Hispanics and the country. It would mean that for the first time a major ethnic immigrant group, guided by its leaders, had eschewed the path of assimilation. Every previous group—Germans, Irish, Italians, Greeks, Jews, Poles—struggled to be accepted fully into the social, political, and economic mainstream, sometimes against the opposition of a hostile majority. They learned the language, acquired education and skills, and adapted their own customs and traditions to fit into an American context. Assimilation proved an effective model for members of these ethnic groups, who now rank among the most successful Americans, as measured by earnings and education. But a quarter of a century ago another model emerged and challenged assimilation as a guide to the behavior of ethnic groups. This model originated in the civil rights movement of the 1960s.

THE CIVIL RIGHTS MODEL

By midcentury it was clear that blacks had not been assimilated into American society as other groups had. Immigrants—even those from southern and eastern Europe, whose appearance, culture, and language set them apart from previous groups that had settled in the United States—had gradually been accepted into the social and economic mainstream.

But blacks had been kept outside it for generations. They remained a separate, distinct, and obviously disadvantaged group. It was clear that a more aggressive policy would have to be pursued if blacks were ever to become full and equal participants in the society. The Civil Rights Act of 1964 was a far-reaching attempt to change the behavior of private individuals, as well as of government bodies. It prohibited discrimination in public accommodations, in employment, and in any programs that received federal funds. Along with laws that prohibited discrimination in voting and education, the act guaranteed that each person should be considered on his or her own merits, without imposing limits or conferring privileges on the basis of race.

Like the assimilation process, civil rights laws promised to blur distinctions between people—at least the invidious ones based on prejudice. Such laws could lift barriers that had prevented blacks and others who suffered discrimination from competing, but they could not, overnight, erase the effects of decades of discrimination. Even if the 1964 Civil Rights Act had immediately eradicated racial discrimination—which of course it did not—it would still have taken a generation or more for blacks to "catch up" in education, earnings, and other measures of social and economic well-being. And there were no guarantees that blacks, or any other group, would succeed as a group; the only guarantee was that individuals would have the right to try to succeed by the same rules that applied to all persons. But rising expectations and impatience drove the civil rights movement to a radical transformation in the 1960s and 1970s.

When equal opportunity did not immediately produce equal results, civil rights leaders shifted away from arguing for a neutral, color-blind process. They insisted instead that the process produce equal outcomes for all groups, which could happen only if society became even more color conscious. Equal opportunity gave way to affirmative action. It was no longer sufficient for employers to guarantee an impartial selection process in hiring or promoting individuals. Federally mandated affirmative action programs, for example, forced employers who received government contracts to set goals for hiring a certain percentage of minorities and women. Race, gender, and national origin once again became important factors in hiring, firing, and promoting employees. The principles of affirmative action were extended to education and even to voting, when blacks (and, later, Hispanics) became entitled to vote in election districts in which they made up the majority of voters.

HISPANICS AND THE NEW ENTITLEMENTS

The changes brought about by the civil rights movement had a profound effect on Hispanics. Unlike blacks, who had been a part of the national consciousness for well over a century, Hispanics were virtually unknown to most Americans and ignored by policy makers and politicians, at least at the national level. In 1960 there were only about seven million Hispanics in the United States, 4 percent of the population. Most of these were either Mexican Americans who had lived in the Southwest for generations, many of whom were poor and uneducated, or Puerto Ricans who had migrated from the island to the Northeast after World War II and were faring poorly, especially in New York. In the decade after 1960, one million Cuban refugees fleeing Fidel Castro's Communist revolution in their homeland added to the Hispanic population, settling mostly in southern Florida. These groups were diverse, sharing no history or agenda. Within three decades, however, Hispanics became an important and powerful interest group, whose leaders argued that Hispanics could succeed only by mimicking the strategy of the black civil rights movement.

In the mid-1960s money from the War on Poverty began

to pour into minority communities for self-help programs in education and housing. Schools, universities, and employers began devising special programs aimed at the recruiting of minorities. Foundations, too, were creating projects and forming organizations to help minorities develop their economic and political potential. So long as Hispanics remained a separate and disadvantaged group, they were entitled to affirmative action programs, compensatory education, government set-asides, and myriad other programs. Previous immigrants had been eager to become "American," to learn the language, to fit in. But the entitlements of the civil rights era encouraged Hispanics to maintain their language and culture, their separate identity, in return for the rewards of being members of an officially recognized minority group. Assimilation gave way to affirmative action.

The effect of this change was twofold: it strengthened Hispanic ethnic identity, since entitlement was based on membership in an officially designated minority group; and it placed a premium on disadvantaged status. Hispanic leaders developed a vested interest in showing that Hispanics were, as the head of one Hispanic organization described it, "the poorest of the poor, the most segregated minority in schools, the lowest-paid group in America and the least-educated minority in this nation."[1] Such descriptions justified Hispanics' entitlement to affirmative action programs, but they also created a perverse standard of success. To succeed at the affirmative action game, Hispanics had to establish their failure in other areas. The point of this game was for Hispanics to show that they were making less social and economic progress than other groups and therefore deserved greater assistance. Hispanic leaders, ignoring tangible evidence to the contrary, complained as Representative Edward Roybal (D-Calif.) did: ". . . we are no better off today than we were in 1949."[2] Others invoked the specter of "a permanent Hispanic underclass," as if to ensure no end to Hispanic entitlement.

REAL PROGRESS

Despite the general pessimism of Hispanic leaders, the evidence suggests that Hispanics are making real progress today. What's more, if ever the analogy between blacks and Hispanics was a fair one, it no longer is. Most native-born Hispanics have leaped over blacks in achievement, and those Hispanics who are most disadvantaged are, by and large, recent immigrants. Still, Hispanic leaders insist that all Hispanics, even new immigrants, should be entitled to affirmative action programs and other ethnic entitlements that are the legacy of the civil rights movement. What these leaders fail to acknowledge is that Hispanics are succeeding as most other groups before them did, by acquiring the education and skills to advance in this society. Even newcomers, who start off on the bottom rungs of the economic ladder, climb quickly. Within one or two generations living in the United States, the great majority of Hispanics are integrated into the social and economic mainstream.

The story of Hispanic progress and achievement is largely untold. Hispanics are still regarded and treated as a permanently disadvantaged minority. Their leaders seem more intent on vying with blacks for permanent victim status than on seeking recognition for genuine progress by Hispanics over the last three decades. The purpose of this book is to tell the story of that progress. But it is also to warn that attempts to keep Hispanics outside the mainstream of this society—speaking their own language, living in protected enclaves, entitled to privileges based on disadvantage—could derail that progress.

Ultimately, individual Hispanics will choose whether they wish to become part of the larger society or remain separate from it, but public policy can and does influence that choice. Chapters 1 and 2 show how public policy in the form of two federal laws, the Bilingual Education Act and the Voting Rights Act, encouraged Hispanics to reject assimilation.

Chapter 1 traces the history of bilingual education in the Hispanic community, which began as a program to help children learn English and ended up a multimillion dollar program to preserve Hispanics' native language and culture. Chapter 2 details how a law originally designed to stop southern states from denying blacks the right to vote was transformed into one that allows Hispanics to cast ballots in Spanish in federal elections and guarantees the creation of majority Hispanic electoral districts. Chapter 3 describes how the organizations involved in promoting these policies evolved and how groups outside the Hispanic community influenced the process. Chapter 4 considers the backlash that developed as Hispanic leaders continued to push for special treatment, including protected language rights for Hispanics.

The second half of the book deals with the present condition of Hispanics living in the United States. Chapter 5 shows that native-born Hispanics are moving into the economic mainstream and explains why most analysts fail to recognize this phenomenon. Chapter 6 describes Hispanic immigration, which is becoming the predominant feature of the Hispanic population. While most Hispanics, including Latin immigrants, are making progress, one group of Hispanics is slipping further behind. Chapter 7 examines why Puerto Ricans are failing and what role public policy has played in discouraging Puerto Rican achievement.

The concluding chapter outlines my thoughts on why Hispanics must adopt a new politics of assimilation. There is no reason to believe that Hispanics cannot mimic the success of many other ethnic groups in becoming full participants in the social, political, and economic life of this nation. But they will not do so by ignoring the lessons of the past.

CHAPTER 1

The Bilingual Battleground

For more than a hundred years, the struggle to assimilate immigrant children was fought in public school classrooms. Millions of Germans, Italians, Poles, Jews, Greeks, and others entered school speaking a foreign tongue, unfamiliar with the habits of their new culture, and were transformed there. For the overwhelming majority of these immigrant children, learning English was the first and most crucial step on the road to becoming "American." The process was sometimes cruel and always difficult, and not everyone succeeded—but most did. Today, the schools are again being used as agents of social change, this time with Hispanic children. The purpose is not to assimilate Hispanic children, however, but to maintain and strengthen their ethnic identity by teaching them in their native language and by inculcating in them their native culture. In the process, these children have become the most segregated students in American public schools, kept apart from their English-speaking peers even after they have acquired basic English skills, sometimes for years. The history of bilingual education in the Hispanic community is marked by false hope and intrigue; it is a case study in the use of legislative, judicial, and administrative authority to promote an unpopular policy among an unsuspecting public.

A MODEST PROPOSAL

Bilingual education marked the first salvo in Hispanics' war to preserve their ethnic identity. But when the program was initiated more than twenty years ago, there was little hint that it would become a major diversion from the path of assimilation. In 1960 Spanish was still the dominant language of the Hispanic population, which was already large, at seven million persons, and growing. Many of these Hispanics were not immigrants but native-born Americans: Mexican Americans, whose families had lived in what is now the southwest United States for centuries, and Puerto Ricans, U.S. citizens by birth, about one million of whom migrated to the mainland after World War II.[1] Yet many Mexican American and Puerto Rican children—perhaps half—could not speak English when they entered the first grade.[2] Many were held behind; some were put into classes for the retarded; others (perhaps as many as 80 percent) eventually dropped out of school.

A few school districts had programs for non-English-speaking children, but most did not. The most common special program, English as a Second Language (ESL), emphasized instruction in English, with students spending one or more periods a day being taught basic English skills in classes and the rest of the day learning other subjects in regular classes. Only about 5 percent of all Hispanic children were enrolled in such programs in 1969.[3] By far the majority of students who did not speak English at the time were allowed to sink or swim in classrooms that offered no special instruction. Educators and Hispanic leaders were eager for any new ideas on how to improve the education of these severely disadvantaged Mexican American and Puerto Rican students. They found one in bilingual education, a program developed to meet the needs of far more privileged Hispanic youngsters.

In 1960 Dade County, Florida, public schools were inundated with Cuban children, whose mostly middle-class and wealthy parents had settled in Florida after fleeing their homeland in the wake of Fidel Castro's Communist revolution in 1959. Most of the refugees anticipated that their stay would be temporary. Their desire was to oust Castro and return to their homeland. In the meantime, their children attended local public schools, which were given special federal assistance to meet their special needs, especially in language development. In 1961 one local school began a special program of instruction in Spanish for Spanish speakers, developed with the help of Cuban-trained educators anxious that Cuban youngsters not lose their Spanish skills. The program was expanded two years later to a full-fledged bilingual program for elementary students, which was replicated in other schools in the district.

Children learned their lessons in Spanish half the day and in English the other half. According to an evaluation of the program conducted by the school system in 1966, children in the bilingual program performed as well as or better than comparable children in monolingual English schools.[4] Proponents of bilingual education concluded that the method held promise for educating disadvantaged Hispanic youngsters as well. They called for a national program to encourage school districts to teach Hispanic children their regular lessons in Spanish while they learned English so that they would not fall behind. The idea had simple and direct appeal; all that was needed was a way to encourage school districts to implement it. Bilingual education advocates found a champion for their cause in Senator Ralph Yarborough, a liberal Democrat from Texas.

In 1967 Yarborough introduced legislation to provide federal aid for bilingual education for poor Mexican American children in public schools. His aim, Yarborough said, was "not to keep any specific language alive. It is not the purpose of the bill to create pockets of different languages through the country ... not to stamp out the mother tongue and not to try to make their mother tongue the dominant language, but just to try to make those children fully literate in English."[5] The legislation did not attempt to define bilingual education. According to the education historian Diane Ravitch, "the vagueness of the legislation was intentional. Yarborough candidly admitted that 'Every time people ask me, "What does bilingual education mean?" I reply that it means different things to different people.' "[6] The one key element that distinguished bilingual education from other approaches was its emphasis on the child's native language. Despite some congressional opposition to the idea of teaching non-English-speaking children in their native language and a general lack of enthusiasm on the part of the Johnson administration, the measure passed after a series of hearings in California, Texas, and New York mustered political support in the Hispanic community for the proposal.

The Bilingual Education Amendments became Title VII of the Elementary and Secondary Education Act in 1968, providing limited federal funds ($7.5 million in the first year) for local demonstration projects to teach economically disadvantaged children by means of bilingual methods. Today, the total federal contribution to various bilingual education programs exceeds $750 million yearly, and Senator Yarborough's Title VII program alone accounts for $170 million.[7] But more important than the growth in funding has been the dramatic transformation of the goal of bilingual education from that of providing remedial help for disadvantaged Hispanic children to that of fostering ethnic identity and group pride.

For anyone who cared to notice, the seeds for this transformation were planted during the hearings on Senator Yarborough's original bill. Although the senator maintained that the purpose of his legislation was to help Mexican American children become literate in English, most of the testimony in support of his bill argued for an entirely different agenda.

Witness after witness testified that the abysmal educational achievement of Hispanics was due to a public school system hostile to Hispanic culture. Ravitch has written,

Four assumptions, which were usually stated as facts rather than as assumptions, dominated the hearings: first, that Hispanic children did poorly in school because they had a "damaged self-concept"; second, that this negative self-appraisal occurred because the child's native tongue was not the language of instruction; third, that the appropriate remedy for this problem was bilingual instruction; and fourth, that children who were taught their native language (or their *parents'* native language) and their cultural heritage would acquire a positive self-concept, high self-esteem, better attitudes toward school, increased motivation, and improved educational achievement.[8]

These arguments were being advanced not only in education and political circles but also on the streets. Hispanic protesters in Los Angeles, San Antonio, Albuquerque, and Denver, as well as in smaller communities like Uvalde County, Texas, demanded that school districts adopt bilingual and bicultural education for Hispanic children. In March 1968 Mexican American high school students in Los Angeles staged a massive school walkout, demanding that the board of education institute compulsory bilingual-bicultural education for all Mexican American students. Although the board did not immediately agree to the students' demands, it did respond by "recogniz[ing] that it is highly desirable to provide some degree of bilingual-bicultural education for Spanish surnamed students."[9] Within two years of passage of Senator Yarborough's modest proposal to help Hispanic children learn English, bilingual education had become the symbol of ethnic solidarity for Hispanic activists. But it would still take the actions of the federal bureaucracy and the courts to turn this symbol of ethnic pride into a guaranteed civil right.

BILINGUAL EDUCATION AND EQUAL RIGHTS

The transformation began in the Office for Civil Rights (OCR) of the Department of Health, Education, and Welfare, which was responsible for ensuring nondiscrimination in education programs. The Civil Rights Act of 1964 prohibited any program receiving federal funds from discriminating against persons on the basis of national origin as well as race. School districts, which began receiving federal funds for the first time in 1965 under the Elementary and Secondary Education Act, now found themselves subject to unprecedented federal oversight of their education programs. In 1970 OCR issued guidelines for school districts whose enrollment exceeded 5 percent Hispanic or other national-origin minority groups. The guidelines said that such school districts should take "affirmative steps" to help non-English-speaking children participate effectively in the educational program offered by the school district.[10]

Unlike the Bilingual Education Act, which was purely voluntary, the OCR directive was compulsory. School districts with even a small percentage of non-English-speaking students would have to come up with programs to address the needs of these students if they were to continue to receive any federal funds. The first test of the guidelines came in 1974 in a California case involving a Chinese student, Kinney Lau, who attended a school in San Francisco that offered no special help to non-English-speaking students like him. The case ultimately went to the Supreme Court, which declared that non-English-speaking children had a constitutionally protected right to special language programs. "There is no equality of treatment merely by providing students with the same facilities, textbooks, teachers, and curriculum; for students who do not understand English are effectively foreclosed from any meaningful education," the Court said. The Court stopped short of dictating what kind of programs schools would have to institute in order to comply with their order: "Teaching English to the students of Chinese ancestry who do not speak the language is one choice. Giving instruction to the group in Chinese is another. There may be others."[11] But OCR quickly stepped into the breach.

Armed with the *Lau* decision, OCR established a series of guidelines in 1975 that prescribed how local school districts would deal with what it now termed "language minority" children. The "Lau remedies," as they came to be known, were written by an appointed task force made up largely of bilingual education advocates. Not surprisingly, the task force determined that bilingual education—providing instruction in the child's native language and native culture—was the sole acceptable method to teach most language minority children. Notwithstanding the Court's admonition that native language instruction was but one choice available to school districts, OCR rejected other methods. It prohibited English as a Second Language (ESL) instruction for elementary or intermediate school children and insisted that high school children be offered supplementary programs in addition to ESL. OCR also went beyond the Supreme Court ruling in determining who had a right to mandatory bilingual education. The Court had addressed only the right of non-English-speaking students to special instruction so that they could benefit from the school's program. OCR, however, extended the requirement for bilingual education to all children who came from homes in which English was not the primary language spoken. School districts were required to determine what language was most often used in the child's home, what language the child used most frequently, and what language the child learned first. Whether children from such homes understood English and could benefit from an English-language school curriculum was more or less irrelevant under the Lau remedies.[12]

Between 1975 and 1980 OCR negotiated five hundred plans mandating bilingual education in local school districts that had at least twenty students from a single language group. While OCR retreated slightly from its position that bilingual education was the *only* acceptable method of teaching language minority students, it still required school districts wishing to use alternative methods to prove that such methods were superior to bilingual education. School districts were faced with a clear choice: initiate bilingual programs, whose effectiveness did not have to be demonstrated, or accept the burden of proving the superior effectiveness of alternative programs. Most school districts simply acceded to the clear intention of OCR, which was to provide a virtual monopoly for bilingual instruction. Several states promptly adopted bilingual education laws and provided money for their implementation.

The claim that Hispanics had a right to bilingual education under civil rights laws and the Constitution was frequently advanced in state and federal courts, as well. Like that in the *Lau* case, early suits on behalf of Hispanic students pitted bilingual advocates against school districts that offered no programs, or only minimal ones, for non-English-speaking students. In the wake of the OCR guidelines, suits were being filed by plaintiffs who argued that even if school districts offered special help, such as intensive English-language instruction, they were nonetheless depriving Hispanic children of equal educational opportunity. A federal court declared that Hispanic students in Portales, New Mexico, were being denied their right to equal protection under the Fourteenth Amendment because the school system did not provide bilingual education for *all* Hispanic students. The same principle was articulated by a federal court in Texas, which ruled that the state must provide bilingual education to all students with limited proficiency in English. Although the Texas ruling was overturned by a federal appeals court, which ruled that Congress had not explicitly called on states to provide bilingual education for all non-English-speaking students, the state of Texas passed legislation mandating bilingual education in school districts where more than twenty students in the same grade had limited proficiency in English.[13] Suits on behalf of bilingual education were by no means limited to Mexican Americans. In 1974 Puerto Rican plaintiffs won a consent decree that guaranteed bilingual instruction for New York City's 150,000 Hispanic students; and in Patchogue-Medford, New York, a federal district court struck down a program for Hispanic youngsters, which provided only special ESL instruction and failed to teach them about their native culture.[14]

All of these cases advanced the idea that bilingual and, especially, bicultural education were good for Hispanic children, regardless of whether they could already speak English. This was a far cry from the original purpose of the Bilingual Education Act, which was simply to help non-English-speaking children learn how to read and write, to add and subtract, in their native language while they learned English. When the act came up for reauthorization in 1973, however, Congress gave its stamp of approval to this new direction.

With the defeat of Senator Yarborough in 1970, the task of shepherding bilingual education legislation through the Congress fell to Senators Alan Cranston (D-Calif.), Edward Kennedy (D-Mass.), and Joseph Montoya (D-N.M.). From the beginning it was clear that bilingual advocates wanted more than a simple reauthorization of Title VII, which was what the Nixon administration proposed. Senate sponsors favored an expansion of the program, which would make it available to middle-class children and require bicultural education in addition to native-language instruction. Senator Montoya, who represented New Mexico, home to the oldest and proportionately largest Hispanic population of any state, was the most outspoken champion of expanding bilingual education. In a memo to the Senate committee considering legislation reauthorizing the act, Senator Montoya wrote, "It is wrong to assume that all bicultural children speak English poorly or that they do not need the assistance of this act if they already speak English well or fairly well. . . . However, the sense of the bill is that bilingual ability is an advantage and that the ability to speak, *read and write*, in both languages is needed to fully educate these children."[15] Others urged that bicultural education be incorporated in the legislation as well. The deputy staff director of the U.S. Commission on Civil Rights, Louis Nuñez, suggested "the term 'bilingual-bicultural education' be used instead of 'bilingual education,' " so that no one would mistake the program for remedial education for non-English-speaking children.[16]

Although Congress did not incorporate bicultural education into the title of the legislation it passed, the program requirements were modified to include a cultural component. The new law also deleted references to low-income families and did not require participants to be non-English-speaking themselves. These changes encouraged the enrollment of more middle-class Hispanics who were fluent in English, because it was assumed that such children would benefit from learning about their native culture. In one key area, however, Congress began to apply the brakes: it set limits on the amount of native-language instruction that could take place in federally funded Title VII bilingual programs (although OCR could continue to insist that states fund native-language instruction or be in violation of civil rights laws). The House conferees in the final negotiations added language to the legislation that limited the use of children's native language "to the extent necessary to allow children to progress effectively through the education system."[17] Some members of Congress, at least, were not ready to make bilingual education strictly a native-language maintenance program for Hispanic children.

THE FIRST CRITICAL RUMBLINGS

Most supporters of bilingual education in the Congress, the bureaucracy, and the courts believed that the program offered some educational benefit to children whose first language was not English. After all, Hispanic leaders and educators claimed that the program was best for their children. This was taken as an article of faith by most Hispanic educators and accepted as fact by policy makers. It came as a rude shock in 1977 when the first comprehensive evaluation of federally funded bilingual programs showed them to be largely ineffective in teaching English, allowing students to keep up with other subjects in their native language, or improving students' sense of self-esteem.

The release of the report, written by the American Institutes for Research (AIR), set off an acrimonious debate among education researchers that continues to this day. The AIR study sampled 286 classrooms in all thirty-eight Spanish/English projects that had been operating for at least four years. The findings were explosive: children in the programs scored more poorly on tests of English proficiency than comparable students who were not enrolled in bilingual education, and scored no better than such students in math. Not only were students in bilingual education failing to learn English as rapidly as those outside the program, but they were not learning other subjects any better. The whole point of bilingual education, supporters had claimed initially, was to help Hispanic children keep up with math and other basic subjects while they learned English. The AIR bilingual students tested at about the 30th percentile in math when compared with national norms—no better than their Hispanic peers who had been taught only in English. Bilingual education also seemed to have little impact on how Hispanic students felt about school. Neither the students in bilingual programs nor those not enrolled in such programs indicated strong positive or negative attitudes toward school.[18]

Even more damaging to the program's credibility was AIR's finding that two-thirds of the Hispanic children enrolled in bilingual education were already proficient in English. An astonishing 86 percent of all bilingual project directors interviewed by AIR admitted that they kept Hispanic children in the program after they had learned English. These project directors were simply putting into practice the goal that Hispanic leaders had been advocating since the inception of bilingual education: the maintenance of native language and culture. As one of those leaders told a congressional committee in 1970,

The Mexican American has set his sights on the reform of the public school system in the Southwest.... No longer will he put up with educators who promote a monolingual, monocultural society.... He wants his children Americanized, but not anglicized; he believes that the Mexican American child can learn and that his language should not be an obstacle to his success, but an effective tool for learning and that to destroy it is to destroy his identity and self esteem.[19]

The AIR study showed that Hispanic children in the bilingual program were not learning English or math very well, but they were learning Spanish. The only area in which they surpassed those not in the program was in reading Spanish.

The idea that bilingual education was at its heart a program to help maintain the language and culture of Hispanic children rather than an aid to teaching them English caused great concern among some members of Congress. Barely three years earlier, Congress had rebuffed a move by some members (most notably, Senator Montoya) to make bilingual education a native-language and cultural maintenance program. The AIR report showed that bilingual education project directors were ignoring congressional intent. The directors clearly believed that one of the program's purposes—if not its chief purpose—was to teach Hispanic children about their own culture and to do so in their native language.

On the heels of the AIR report, another critique of bilingual education took aim at some of the program's cherished assumptions. Noel Epstein, an editor at the *Washington Post*, published *Language, Ethnicity, and the Schools: Policy Alternatives for Bilingual-Bicultural Education* in 1977 while on leave to George Washington University's Institute for Educational Leadership.[20] Epstein questioned whether it was appropriate federal policy to require local school districts to promote native-language maintenance and ethnic ties among certain groups—most notably Hispanics. He did not challenge the right of members of an ethnic group to promote and retain their own language and culture in their homes or through their churches and civic groups, only whether it made sense for government—particularly the federal government—to do it for them.

Others were raising similar questions, sparked by concerns less about bilingual education than about the whole ethnic revival movement that had sprung up since the late 1960s. Ethnic heritage programs had proliferated in colleges and public schools, leading one expert on ethnicity, the Massachusetts Institute of Technology professor emeritus Harold Isaacs, to ask,

What is the responsibility of schools maintained by every one's taxes? What is the balance to be struck between what is common to all and what is particular to some? In dealing with the many particulars, who decides, and on what basis, *whose* version of any particular heritage is to be studied? How far can any such program be carried beyond inclusive and reasonably objective treatments provided to all for the benefit and knowledge of all? What justification is there for spending public funds on the active promotion of any single brand of any particular ethnic identification among its own presumed communicants?[21]

Isaacs's questions were particularly relevant at a time when the "culture" being taught in public school programs to promote ethnicity was not merely the history, customs, and traditions of various ethnic groups. Many ethnic studies programs challenged traditional values, arguing that minority children should not be expected to accept middle-class white definitions of right and wrong. A pamphlet entitled *Fostering a Pluralistic Society through Multi-Ethnic Education*, published in 1978 for the Phi Delta Kappa Education Foundation, for example, argued that minority children should not be reprimanded for copying the work of fellow students. Such children, the author claimed, were brought up in communities in which all property, including intellectual property or knowledge, was shared. Insensitive teachers who reprimanded them were arbitrarily and viciously denying these children's cultural heritage:

Almost daily, many students in American public schools experience assaults like this on their ethnic values. Quietly, they adjust to these assaults, corral their beliefs, and suppress their feelings.... Teachers do not understand ethnicity. Teachers neither know, nor have they been taught, that ethnicity, racism, and ethnocentrism are endemic factors in American society that influence teaching and learning.[22]

Such views were popular among some education reformers in the late 1970s, but they found little resonance among politicians. By 1978, when the Bilingual Education Act was once again up for reauthorization, reaction to the excesses of the program had begun to set in. James Crawford, former Washington editor of *Education Week*, has noted, "Even President Jimmy Carter, who liked to show off his own knowledge of Spanish and who had appointed officials favorable to bilingual maintenance programs, told his Cabinet: 'I want English taught, not ethnic culture.' "[23]

When the 1978 amendments were finally adopted, however, only nominal restrictions were put in place. For the first time, the term "transitional bilingual education" was used, signaling that legislators did not want the program to become a native-language maintenance program. Yet the definitions that determined who would be eligible to participate once again expanded the pool. The 1968 and 1974 amendments were aimed at children of "limited English speaking ability," but the 1978 amendments permitted children to remain in the program even after their speaking skills were adequate, so long as they demonstrated difficulty in reading and writing English.[24] One of the chief criticisms in the AIR evaluation was that most of the children in bilingual programs were English speakers; but instead of forbidding this practice in the 1978 amendments, Congress actually created the first legislative basis for their inclusion.

BILINGUAL PROPONENTS OVERREACH

For more than a decade, every time bilingual education came up for reauthorization, it expanded not just in size but also in scope. In 1968 Congress envisioned a program for poor Mexican American children who couldn't speak English. In 1974 Congress decided middle-class Hispanic children could benefit by learning their native language and about their native culture and so included them. In 1978 Congress explicitly made allowance for children who already spoke English, Hispanic and non-Hispanic. Meanwhile, mounting evidence failed to show bilingual education to be the most effective means to teach non-English-speaking children. Critics of the program hoped that the election of Ronald Reagan as president would bring about a change in bilingual education policy.

In the waning days of the 1980 presidential election, the Carter administration decided to issue regulations giving the so-called Lau remedies the force of law. The action was spurred in part by a federal suit by an Alaskan school district that objected to OCR requirements that it institute native-language instruction for its indigenous populations or face the loss of federal funds. The district contended that OCR had never actually issued regulations to implement the Lau decision and that the guidelines did not have the force of law. The underlying objection, however, was that the district was being forced to institute native-language literacy programs for indigenous languages that had no written form in order to serve children who often did not speak their "native" language. OCR's solution to this conundrum was to order the school district to do what was necessary to comply with the OCR directives. In order to meet OCR's objections, the district would have had to hire linguists to help devise an alphabet so that the children in question could not only learn to speak the language of their parents but to do something even their parents couldn't: read and write the language as well. The suit was settled when OCR issued proposed regulations in August 1980, but the issue was far from closed.

Reaction to the proposed regulations was swift and unequivocal. The education community—almost without exception—was outraged by the regulations, which went even further in mandating bilingual education than the guidelines had. The Department of Education received nearly five thousand written comments from the public, and Congress responded by blocking implementation of the regulations until mid-1981. The chief objection to the regulations was that the Department of Education was attempting to dictate classroom policy from Washington. Even those organizations that had traditionally supported funding for bilingual education programs found it difficult to countenance the unprecedented federal intrusion into the pedagogical practices of local classrooms that the regulations would have required.

The new Reagan administration acted quickly to quell the

furor by withdrawing the regulations within days of the president's inauguration. But before the regulations were withdrawn, officials within the Education Department initiated an important review of research on bilingual education that would ultimately wrack the bilingual education research community. Ironically, the review of research came at the behest of the Carter White House Regulatory Analysis and Review Group, which asked for an assessment of the effectiveness of transitional bilingual education in conjunction with the proposed regulations.

QUESTIONING THE EFFECTIVENESS OF BILINGUAL EDUCATION

The researchers Keith Baker and Adriana de Kanter, both career employees of the Department of Education's Office of Planning, Budget, and Evaluation, decided to focus on two questions:

1. Does transitional bilingual education lead to better performance in English?
2. Does transitional bilingual education lead to better performance in nonlanguage subject areas?

In their review, Baker and de Kanter looked at more than three hundred bilingual education studies from around the world. Most studies were so flawed in their methodology, however, that Baker and de Kanter rejected them. Only thirty-nine studies met minimally acceptable research standards, so the published review focused on these.[25]

In this, the most extensive review of research literature on bilingual education ever, Baker and de Kanter concluded,

The case for the effectiveness of transitional bilingual education is so weak that exclusive reliance on this instructional method is clearly not justified. Too little is known about the problems of educating language minorities to prescribe a specific remedy at the Federal level. There-fore, while meeting civil rights guarantees, each school district should decide what type of special program is most appropriate for its own unique setting.

There is not justification for assuming that it is necessary to teach nonlanguage subjects in the child's native tongue in order for the language-minority child to make satisfactory progress in school....

The entire rationale for requiring bilingual education for children with limited English proficiency was undermined by the Baker/de Kanter report.

For years bilingual education advocates argued not only that bilingual education was an effective way to teach non-English-speaking children but that it was the most effective method—indeed, the only acceptable method. Government officials unquestioningly adopted this view, with scant re-search to back up the claims. The AIR study in 1977 had exposed problems within federally funded bilingual educa-tion programs, and the Epstein monograph had questioned whether promoting attachment to native language and cul-ture was appropriate federal policy—but Baker and de Kan-ter's study amounted to a broadside on bilingual education theory. Baker and de Kanter, after all, were reviewing re-search on bilingual education in other countries as well as the United States, on programs aimed at children from lan-guage majority as well as language minority groups.

Baker and de Kanter found that many studies that had claimed promising results for bilingual education were so flawed that they provided little useful information. Of the acceptable studies, they concluded, eleven showed positive outcomes in teaching English for transitional bilingual education programs, fifteen showed no difference, and five actually suggested a negative effect on English acquisition.[26]

CIRCLING THE WAGONS

Bilingual education advocates have responded to the Baker/de Kanter review with great defensiveness. They have spent enormous amounts of time and resources in the last ten years trying to refute it. But even the most favorable reevaluation of the Baker/de Kanter research has shown only small to moderate positive effects favoring bilingual instruction.[27] Advocates of bilingual education approach the issue with almost religious fervor. For them the world is divided into two camps: believers and nonbelievers. Anyone even mildly skeptical of the efficacy of bilingual education is branded a heretic. When the evidence suggests that bilingual education has been less than an unqualified success, advocates attribute any problems to inadequate implementation: bilingual education fails to produce perfect results because there are no perfect programs. Few advocates are as candid as Kenji Hakuta, an associate professor at Yale and an enthusiastic supporter of bilingual education:

There is a sober truth that even the ardent advocate of bilingual education would not deny. Evaluation studies of the effectiveness of bilingual education in improving either English or math scores have not been overwhelmingly in favor of bilingual education. To be sure, there are programs that have been highly effective, but not very many. In a short monograph titled "Research Evidence for the Effectiveness of Bilingual Education," for example, Rudolf Troike (1978) listed about a dozen of them. An awkward tension blankets the lack of empirical demonstration of the success of bilingual education programs. Someone promised bacon, but it's not there.[28]

Faced with poor evaluations of bilingual programs, advocates have recently decided to argue their cause on theoretical rather than on practical grounds. The most influential theorists are James Cummins and Stephen Krashen. According to their theories, children are less likely to develop proficiency in a second language until they have a certain degree of proficiency in their first language. They favor keeping children in native-language programs for extended periods, ideally six years. Cummins also believes that children are incapable of learning new concepts in a second language until at least eight years of age. Actual experience, however, provides little support for Cummins's and Krashen's theories.[29] Literally millions of immigrant children in the United States and elsewhere have managed to acquire proficiency in a second language at a very early age, most without any special help. Cummins's and Krashen's theories, however, do support the political objectives of bilingual advocates, who want Hispanic youngsters to have the opportunity to be kept in bilingual programs until they learn Spanish well enough to become functioning bilinguals. This view was summed up well by Eduardo Hernandez-Chavez at a bilingual education conference sponsored by Georgetown University:

... the school, as one of the most influential institutions of acculturation in our society, bears great responsibility either in the maintenance of the language and culture of Chicanos or in the shift to Anglo American norms. It cannot remain aloof from this process. It must either work as an agent of deculturation and assimilation, or it must work actively and positively with the ethnic communities to support and develop their language and culture in the education of their children. . . .

We urgently need to seek a policy of bilingualism in this country that supports the maintenance, development, and full flowering of the ethnic languages. Moreover, this must be done in a way that not only encourages a personal and individual bilingualism, but beyond this, promotes the learning and use of the ethnic language in such a way that it is maintained strong within the community. Such a policy can only be beneficial, both to the ethnic groups themselves and to the wider society as a whole.[30]

Hernandez-Chavez's views can be heard frequently among professional bilingual educators. At the National Association for Bilingual Education convention in 1984, for example, virtually every speaker advocated an official policy of bilingualism in the United States.[31] There is little evidence that Hispanic parents believe that the purpose of bilingual education is to help their children retain their native language, however. As one Hispanic college professor wrote in an opinion piece for a Hispanic magazine, "I would like my daughters to be bilingual, but I do not want bilingual training to interfere with their command of English."[32] A study by the Educational Testing Service for the U.S. Department of Education found that the overwhelming majority of Hispanic parents—78 percent of Mexican Americans and 82 percent of Cubans—opposed teaching the child's native language if it meant less time for teaching English.[33] Most Hispanic parents also indicated that they think it is the family's responsibility to teach children about their native culture, not the school's. Still, Hispanic parents are more likely to support bilingual education over alternative teaching methods than other groups such as Asians are, which is not surprising given the nearly universal support for bilingual education among Hispanic leaders and educators.

Whether or not Hispanic parents want bilingual education for their children, many Hispanic children are placed in programs purely on the basis of their ethnicity. When one of my own children entered school in the District of Columbia, I was notified that he would be placed in a bilingual program.

Apparently the school assumed that since his name was Pablo and his mother's name was Chavez, he needed instruction in Spanish. They did not bother to ascertain that English was his first and only language. I informed the school that I did not wish him to be put into bilingual classes, but many parents are not so assertive.

In 1988 Congress prohibited the apparently widespread practice of placing Hispanic children in federally funded bilingual classes simply on the basis of their Spanish surnames. But most bilingual programs operate under specific state bilingual education laws as well as federal law; eleven states have laws that require bilingual education for certain students. In a survey of the ten states with the largest number of bilingual students, Desdemona Cardoza found that most used a survey to determine whether a child should be placed in a bilingual classroom.[34] Although the specific wording of the surveys varies, the information most consistently sought is which language is spoken in the home, not necessarily by the child but by the family.

In Houston, for example, a child may be placed in a bilingual classroom if his parents indicate that a language other than English is most often used by the child *or* most often spoken by others in the home.[35] Once the child has been identified as needing bilingual education, parents are notified by letter. They are assured, "The goal of this program of instruction is to help your child learn English more easily and effectively."[36] Parents are required to sign a receipt of notification, but they are not told that they may choose to withdraw their child, although programs in some states are more careful to inform parents of their rights. An Ohio handbook warns administrators, "Although a child may be identified as a potential limited English proficient student needing bilingual program services, personnel must be sensitive to those parents who are not interested in this type of placement for their child."[37]

FEDERAL RETRENCHMENT
AND LOCAL EXPANSION

After years of congressional wrangling and mounting criticism of the effectiveness of bilingual education, the political issues that have fueled debate have not been resolved. Congress made substantial changes in the Bilingual Education Act in 1988 to allow more English instruction in federally funded programs, but state and local governments seem to be moving in the opposite direction, encouraging children to remain in native-language programs for longer periods and making such programs more widely accessible to all Hispanic youngsters, regardless of whether they already have some command of English.

The 1988 bilingual amendments for the first time opened up substantial federal bilingual education funds (25 percent of the total) to be used for programs that did not rely on native-language instruction, such as English immersion programs. The formula was arrived at by way of an interesting bit of logic. Under the amendments to Title VII passed in 1984, 4 percent of the bilingual funds could be awarded to programs that did not use the native language. (All Title VII funds are awarded on a competitive basis.) Department of Education officials soon discovered that approximately one-fourth of all grant applicants were applying to use these newly approved nonbilingual approaches, even though applicants knew that only 4 percent of all bilingual funds would be awarded to nonbilingual programs. Since one-quarter of all applicants were competing for just 4 percent of the money, Congress reasoned that it should change the allocation formula to allot one-fourth of the money for nonbilingual approaches under the new law. It remains to be seen whether competition for this expanded pot will continue to be keener than for the traditional transitional bilingual program funds.

Bilingual education as the only alternative for teaching lan-guage minority children is becoming even more entrenched at the state and local level. For example, the Los Angeles Uni-fied School District has adopted sweeping changes in pro-grams that will significantly expand bilingual programs. The New York State Education Department has similarly ex-panded bilingual education. In both places, the expanded program will make state-supported bilingual education avail-able from prekindergarten through high school.

The New York model includes other controversial changes in the bilingual education program. The program proposed by the state regents would allow language minority children to take state-mandated exams for high school graduation in their native language "wherever necessary."[38] According to the state bilingual education director, Carmen Perez Hogan, the native-language exams will be given only to children who entered the New York public education system after the eighth grade and is intended to help recent immigrants who may have completed most of their education in their native country. Language minority children will be tested (in their native language) for the same content in math, social studies, and so on, as other children in the system will. They will be held to a different standard of English competence, however. Perez Hogan contends it would be inappropriate to penalize recent immigrants by denying them a diploma solely because they lack sufficient English to pass all of their exams in En-glish. Others, including potential employers, might argue that a New York public school diploma that fails to establish that the recipient is fluent in English is a misleading indicator of student achievement.

The regents' policy statement also commits New York to making bilingual education available to *all* students, regard-less of language background: ". . . it shall be the policy of the Regents that all students in New York State will be encouraged to become fully bilingual (proficient in a second language), and knowledgeable about and sensitive to other cultures."

One of the most controversial elements of the New York plan is the requirement that bilingual education be available for all language minority students who score below the 40th percentile of a standardized English reading test. The previous trigger was a score below the 23rd percentile. The use of percentile ranking to determine eligibility in bilingual programs is itself controversial. By definition, 40 percent of *all* students in a national sample who take an English reading test score at or below the 40th percentile. This would be true even if every student taking the test knew only English. Presumably, since some students taking the test in the national sample are not fluent in English, their absolute scores on the test (the ratio of correct to incorrect answers) will be more likely to place them in the lower percentile rankings. Extending the reach of bilingual eligibility to the 40th percentile, however, is guaranteed to include some—perhaps a majority—of the English monolingual Hispanic students in the program. Hispanic students are more likely to come from lower socioeconomic groups and, like poor students of every racial and ethnic group, to do poorly on standardized achievement tests, regardless of their language background.

The Los Angeles plan brought a swift reaction from a teachers' group critical of bilingual education. The organization, Learning English Advocates Drive (LEAD), was formed in 1987. The group mounted a successful effort among union teachers in Los Angeles in 1987 to oppose bilingual education, with 78 percent of the union members voting in a special referendum to instruct their union to negotiate with the school board to replace bilingual education with English-immersion programs. The group's founder, Sally Peterson, was a third-grade teacher for twenty-two years until she began criticizing her school's bilingual program. She believes she was reassigned to a kindergarten class because of her involvement in LEAD. Peterson says she, along with other members of the group, at first strongly favored bilingual education. Her school has become predominantly Hispanic in the last ten years, and she believes that her Hispanic students are being harmed by being placed in mandatory bilingual education classes.

One of Peterson's chief complaints regards student placement. She maintains that Hispanic students who have enough English to benefit from an all-English instructional program, particularly a structured English-immersion approach that compensates for the child's limited vocabulary, are being put into Spanish-language classrooms. Teachers are required to teach reading to these students in Spanish. Many, she claims, still have not progressed beyond the primer level when they reach her third-grade classroom. They end up dysfunctional in two languages, she says. Moreover, they are separated from their non-Hispanic peers.

The charge that bilingual education leads to more segregation of Hispanic students has plagued the program from the beginning. Some of the congressional modifications in the program to allow more English-speaking children to participate were motivated by a desire to decrease the amount of segregation otherwise brought about by the program. Concern over the link between segregation and bilingual education led the Commonwealth of Massachusetts Board of Education to issue a stunning critique of bilingual education in Boston in 1985, charging that "hundreds of Hispanic students are educationally isolated for far longer than contemplated by the Massachusetts Transitional Bilingual Education Law."[39] In regard to many Hispanic students, the report said, "it appears that bilingual programs *both* segregate them *and* fail to teach a substantial proportion of them the skills which, according to the *Lau* decision, are essential."[40]

State law in Massachusetts recommends that students in bilingual programs leave within three years. In Boston, however, substantial numbers of Hispanic students were kept in the program for six or more years. Of Hispanic bilingual students in Boston middle schools, 46 percent had been in the program since kindergarten or first grade. Of Hispanic students in the bilingual program at three high schools, from 26 to 32 percent had been in it six or more years.[41] The Boston program follows the model preferred by many bilingual advocates—late exit, meaning five or more years of bilingual instruction. Krashen and Cummins, theorists whose work heavily influences bilingual education today, both argue that children kept in bilingual programs for extended periods learn more content in their native language and actually acquire a more solid base in English. Neither seemed to be true for students in Boston.

WHAT NEXT?

In the more than twenty years since the federal government began funding bilingual education, the number of non-English-speaking children has burgeoned. The Hispanic population itself has more than doubled; and much of its growth has been from immigration, bringing more Spanish-speaking children into the schools. But the number of non-English-speaking children from other language backgrounds has been increasing rapidly as well, particularly Southeast Asian refugees. By and large, however, the Asian community has not made demands that Asian children be taught in their native language in public schools. The current native-language programs for groups other than Hispanics are few in number. Most Asian parents prefer that their children be taught in English and consider it the parents' responsibility to teach children their native language and culture.[42] The remarkable

achievement of many of these children, who figure disproportionately among the recipients of national academic schol-
arships, testifies to their success in learning English without
benefit of bilingual or native-language instruction. The feats
of these children, who are immigrants or the children of immigrants, are far from exceptional in historical terms. Rapid
social and economic mobility has been the pattern for generations of immigrants; but the key has always been the learning of English in the public schools. Hispanic political leaders
chose to break with that tradition in 1968 and have steadfastly
held to their position.

Some critics of bilingual education maintain that the program exists largely to provide jobs for an already educated
Hispanic elite, who occupy many of the jobs as bilingual
teachers and administrators. Rosalie Pedalino Porter, a former bilingual teacher and administrator, describes in chilling
detail in her book, *Forked Tongue: The Politics of Bilingual Education*, the lengths to which some bilingual bureaucrats will
go to discredit anyone who criticizes bilingual education or
attempts to modify a program's more doctrinaire aspects.
Porter's own career was nearly destroyed when she aban-
doned native-language instruction in a program she administered in Newton, Massachusetts, in favor of one that relied
more heavily on English instruction. The students' achievement actually improved when they were exposed to more
English-language instruction, but state bilingual education officials cut off funding for the program and insisted that the
Newton schools return to teaching children in their native
language.

Porter, like Sally Peterson in California and countless
anonymous teachers in bilingual programs around the country, questions the wisdom of forcing Hispanic youngsters to
learn their lessons in Spanish when they are clearly ready and
willing to learn English. In her book Porter describes the moment she decided that bilingual education was hurting her

students. As an elementary school bilingual teacher, she spent most of her day teaching her students in Spanish. One day she dutifully asked a young boy to identify the color of a box she was pointing to. *"¿Juan, que color es este?"* she asked, and he replied, "Green." *"Verde,"* she corrected the boy, who repeated, "Green." Says Porter, "I came to feel that I was going about things the wrong way around, as if I were deliberately holding back the learning of English."[43]

In my own visits to bilingual programs in California, Virginia, and the District of Columbia, I have witnessed Mexican, Salvadoran, Guatemalan, and other Hispanic children being taught grammar, reading, math, and social science lessons in Spanish, yet nearly all the students exhibited some command of English. In several classrooms, I observed very young Hispanic children working together at their tables speaking English among themselves as their teachers gave directions in Spanish. In some bilingual schools, I watched Hispanic children as young as six or seven years conversing freely in English as they lined up for lunch or playground. Left to choose their language, they spoke exclusively in English—even when no Anglo students were within earshot. Clearly, such children do not need to be taught in Spanish; they are more comfortable with English. Native-language instruction serves only to reinforce their ethnic identity in the face of the inevitable pressure to assimilate.

Many advocates of bilingual education deem this a worthy goal, but most are unwilling to argue their case before the American public on such terms. They fear—correctly, I believe—that public financial support for bilingual education would evaporate if it were presented as a way to preserve the language and culture of a single ethnic group. It is not even clear that Hispanic parents would support bilingual education on such terms. Instead, advocates try to sell the program with the claim that it is both effective in teaching Hispanic children English and necessary to allow Hispanic children to keep up in school as they learn the language. They fight every attempt to experiment with alternative methods that rely less heavily on the native language, as they did recently in Berkeley, California, where they sued the city for using an English-immersion program that produced demonstrably positive academic results for students in all subject areas.[44] So far, the advocates are winning the battle in most places, at least with respect to Hispanic children. The number of Hispanic children in bilingual programs grows each year, as does funding for the programs at the local, state, and federal levels. No other ethnic group, including the 250,000 immigrants who come here from Asia each year, is clamoring for the right to have its language and culture maintained in this country at public expense. Although Hispanics have succeeded in doing so—for the time being—theirs will be a Pyrrhic victory if it is gained at the expense of their ultimate social and economic integration.

CHAPTER 2

Hispanics and the Voting Rights Act

The Voting Rights Act of 1965 has frequently been called the most effective civil rights law ever enacted. Unlike the Civil Rights Act of 1964, whose provisions were broad and applied to all areas of the country, the Voting Rights Act was devised to correct a specific and regional problem of discrimination. For nearly one hundred years, in open defiance of the Constitution and federal civil rights laws, some southern states had denied blacks the right to vote. Civil rights proponents believed that a law was needed that would severely punish those jurisdictions and prevent them from enacting new measures to deny blacks voting rights. The result was a truly radical piece of legislation, which conferred unprecedented authority on the federal government to regulate voting in all elections in certain southern states. The effect was immediate. Within two years, black voter registration in Mississippi, for example, went from about 6 percent to 60 percent.[1] The number of black elected officials in the South increased rapidly as well, from only 100 in 1965 to nearly five thousand by 1989.[2]

Hispanic leaders were anxious to find a way to apply the provisions of the act to jurisdictions where Hispanics lived, hoping to achieve similar spectacular increases in Hispanic political power. There were two problems. The first was a technical one: the law's triggering mechanism was written originally to include only jurisdictions in the Deep South. The second problem was more fundamental: Hispanics had never been subject to the same denial of their basic right to vote that blacks had suffered, and it was unclear that legislators could be persuaded that Hispanics needed the kind of drastic protections that the Voting Rights Act authorized. Within ten years of passage of the original act, however, Hispanics had overcome both obstacles. By 1975 they had won their right to be included in the act when it was expanded to cover more than 375 jurisdictions outside the South. In the process, Hispanics also secured the right to cast ballots printed in Spanish. Today, they are entitled to even more. Along with blacks, they are guaranteed the right to vote in districts in which they constitute a majority of the eligible voters to ensure that they can elect members of their own group to represent them. But in order for this political strategy to work, Hispanics must remain in the barrio. It is a political victory that can be won only at the expense of the ultimate social and economic integration of Hispanics in this society.

EXPANDING COVERAGE

Unlike other civil rights laws, designed to protect the rights of any group that faced discrimination, the Voting Rights Act was originally intended to protect primarily one group— blacks—and only those blacks who lived in the Deep South. The reason for this limitation was simple: no other group had so systematically been denied the right to vote. Every time any effort was made to help blacks exercise their basic right to vote, southern politicians devised new means to keep them from the polls. Clearly, both a new federal voting rights law and a drastic enforcement mechanism were needed to keep recalcitrant southerners from enacting new laws or rules to prevent blacks from voting. The Voting Rights Act established such a mechanism by requiring all covered jurisdictions to submit any changes in voting, no matter how insignificant (even the switching of a polling site from one side of the street to the other), to the U.S. Justice Department or the District Court of the District of Columbia for approval. This provision applied only to those states or political subdivisions that used a literacy test to determine voting eligibility and in which under 50 percent of the voting-age population had voted in the previous presidential election. By design, this criterion captured nearly all offending southern jurisdictions and exempted those outside the Deep South, which had no history of denying blacks the right to vote, even though some employed literacy tests for all voters.

Congress placed great weight on the literacy test for good reason. Literacy tests were used in the South primarily to keep blacks from voting. As Abigail Thernstrom describes in her book *Whose Votes Count? Affirmative Action and the Voting Rights Act*:

In the 1960s southern registrars were observed testing black applicants on such matters as the number of bubbles in a soap bar, the news contained in a copy of the *Peking Daily*, and the definition of terms such as *habeas corpus*. By contrast, even illiterate whites were being registered.[3]

But at the time the Voting Rights Act was enacted, in 1965, literacy tests were still considered a legitimate method of determining fitness to vote, so long as they were applied impartially to all potential voters regardless of color. New York, for example, used a literacy test to determine voter eligibility but had never been accused of applying the test in a discriminatory manner. Nonetheless, Puerto Ricans sought and won a provision in the act that guaranteed their right to satisfy state literacy requirements by demonstrating literacy in Spanish if they had been educated in Spanish-language schools in Puerto Rico. At the time this provision was added, few people thought it would have much consequence other than guaranteeing Puerto Ricans, who are U.S. citizens by birth, the right to vote in states that required proof of literacy, usually in English. This minor provision later proved to be the wedge in the door for Hispanic coverage under the act. The provision and subsequent suits by Puerto Ricans established the principle that holding elections in English was an impediment to Hispanics in voting. It took ten years, however, for the principle to become part of the act itself.

In 1975 Hispanic civil rights leaders decided to try to amend the special provisions of the Voting Rights Act so that jurisdictions with large numbers of Hispanic voters would also be subject to federal oversight. They knew they would be called on to demonstrate that Hispanics faced the same kind of discrimination that blacks had faced in 1965 in the South and that it would be a difficult case to make. Thernstrom reports on the efforts of the Mexican American Legal Defense and Education Fund (MALDEF) to find witnesses who could testify to voting rights abuses:

The search for evidence of Mexican American disenfranchisement began well before the start of the congressional hearings on the proposed amendments [to the Voting Rights Act]. One member of the MALDEF team remembers "being on the phone to Texas with members of the Chicano community, saying, find ... a Fannie Lou Hamer, find ... a really bad little county with ten little stories, find ... someone who's convincing to come up here and testify before Congress ... to convince the Congress and the administration ... to ... change the rules of the game so that Texas will get covered."[4]

There was no question that blacks had been forcibly prevented en masse from voting in many places in the Deep

South before 1965, but no one had ever suggested that Hispanics or any other group faced the same kind of barriers to
political participation. In Texas, the most hostile environment for them, Mexican Americans held many elective offices—including two congressional seats—a feat unthinkable
for blacks in the Deep South in 1965. Nonetheless, Hispanic
leaders were intent on subjecting Texas and other jurisdictions with large Hispanic populations to the requirements of
the act—especially to its preclearance section, which required
federal approval for all voting changes.

The preclearance provision had become a powerful tool in
the hands of civil rights groups. Originally intended to inhibit
recalcitrant southern jurisdictions from erecting new barriers
to black registration, it quickly became a way for civil rights
groups to influence redistricting decisions. The transformation came about when the Supreme Court ruled that

the right to vote can be affected by a dilution of voting power as well
as by an absolute prohibition on casting a ballot. Voters who are
members of a racial minority might well be in the majority in one
district, but in a decided minority in the county as a whole. This
type of change would therefore nullify their ability to elect the candidate of their choice just as would prohibiting some of them from
voting.[5]

The Court's ruling enlarged the meaning of the "right to
vote," interpreting it to mean that blacks were entitled to vote
in districts where they formed a majority. The decision
handed civil rights groups the means to increase blacks' voting strength by challenging redistricting plans and by eliminating multimember districts in areas with sizable black
populations. Civil rights groups opposed at-large voting and
multimember districts because such districts made it more
difficult to elect blacks. If candidates for city offices were
elected by wards rather than at-large, for example, political

lines could be drawn in such a way that smaller, concentrated pockets of black voters would have the opportunity to elect their own candidates.

It was this power to challenge districting plans, at-large elections, and multimember districts that appealed to MAL-DEF and other Hispanic organizations. The tricky issue was how to arrive at a formula that would include states with large Hispanic populations under the special provisions of the Voting Rights Act, which required that reapportionment and other changes be approved by the Justice Department or the courts. As Thernstrom notes in her book, Mexican Americans in the Southwest had a notoriously low voter turnout, but more than low voter participation was required to force inclusion under the special provisions of the act: ". . . some segments of the white population, after all, rarely voted. In the absence of a literacy test, a device that was unquestionably manipulated to screen registrants by race, black or Hispanic disfranchisement could not be inferred."[6]

After several attempts to draft amendments that would include Hispanics, MALDEF hit upon the idea of adapting its arguments to the act's original triggering device: the literacy test. Although Texas and most other states with large Mexican American populations did not use literacy tests, they did print their ballots and other voting materials in English. MALDEF asserted that English ballots were, in effect, literacy tests, used as a means to exclude otherwise qualified voters. This argument had already been made successfully in a suit brought by Puerto Ricans in New York, who alleged that printing ballots and election materials in English in a city with a large Puerto Rican population constituted a discriminatory form of literacy test.[7] Hispanics had finally found their hook.

The final amendments added new criteria to trigger the special provisions of the act. The formula called for jurisdiction to be covered under the special provisions of the act whenever so-called "language minorities" made up 5 percent of the population of a political jurisdiction and voter turnout in the previous presidential election was less than 50 percent of the voting-age population of that jurisdiction. In addition to triggering the preclearance provisions, the amendment required that bilingual ballots be made available for certain named "language minorities" (Spanish-speaking persons, Asians, American Indians, and Alaskan natives) in jurisdictions that met the preceding criteria or in which the literacy rate of these groups fell below that of the general population.

Initially, most mainstream civil rights organizations opposed amending the Voting Rights Act to include Hispanics. They feared that broadening the act would invite opposition in the Congress and that tampering with the trigger mechanism for the act's preclearance provision would attract unwanted attention to the very sections of the act that had proved most useful to their cause. According to Thernstrom, black opposition finally disappeared when the veteran civil rights lawyer Joseph Rauh, Jr., urged the Leadership Confer ence on Civil Rights to accept changes that would permit coverage of Hispanics.

With black opposition removed, the amendments won overwhelming approval in both houses of Congress—despite the almost complete failure of Hispanic organizations to establish that Hispanics faced discrimination in voting in any way comparable to that faced by blacks in the South before 1965. Both the Justice Department and the U.S. Commission on Civil Rights questioned whether Hispanics deserved coverage. The assistant attorney general for civil rights, J. Stanley Pottinger, Jr., testified, "The Department of Justice has concluded that the evidence does not require expansion based on the record currently before us. In other words, that record is not compelling."[8] The Civil Rights Commission noted that statistics on Hispanic voting "do not paint the shocking picture that, for example, 1965 statistics on Mississippi did."[9] Nevertheless, members of the House and Senate judiciary committees, which heard testimony on the Voting Rights Act amendments, accepted uncritically the testimony of MALDEF and other Hispanic witnesses.

No one questioned the logic that English-language ballots were the same thing as southern literacy tests, which had been used for the *sole* purpose of excluding qualified blacks from voting. No one seemed to care that factors other than a language impediment were far more significant in explaining low voting rates among some Hispanic groups. When Senator Barry Goldwater testified that according to the Census Bureau "40 percent of all Spanish origin persons who were not registered in 1974 reported they were not citizens," he was politely ignored, as if the low citizenship rate among the Mexican origin population were irrelevant to their low voting rate.[10] Instead, Hispanic witnesses, including Hispanic members of Congress, insisted on using raw population figures to demonstrate that Hispanics were "underrepresented" among voters and elected officials.

MALDEF's claim that Mexican Americans had been systematically excluded from participating in politics was contradicted by the facts. From at least 1960 on, presidential candidates had aggressively courted Hispanic voters. In Texas, where voting discrimination against Mexican Americans was alleged to have been greatest, Mexican Americans had never been barred from casting their votes in Democratic primaries, as blacks had in the Deep South. Thernstrom maintains that "[Mexican American] votes had become an important source of Democratic power by the late 19th Century."[11] Indeed, the New Mexico state legislature, in which scores of Hispanics had served since New Mexico became a state, in 1912, petitioned the Congress to be exempted from inclusion, noting, "In the counties of New Mexico where most of the people of Spanish descent live, the voter registration and the number of those citizens voting at primary and general election are the largest in the state."[12] Moreover, Mexican American candidates had run for statewide office (with varying degrees of success) in California, Texas, New Mexico, and Arizona. At the time the Voting Rights Act amendments were passed, two Mexican Americans served as governors in the United States, Jerry Apodoca in New Mexico and Raul Castro in Arizona (a state in which Mexican Americans constituted slightly more than 10 percent of the population); one Mexican American was a U.S. senator, Joseph Montoya of New Mexico; and five Hispanics were members of Congress— Henry B. Gonzalez and Eligio ("Kika") de la Garza of Texas, Edward Roybal of California, Manuel Lujan of New Mexico, and Herman Badillo of New York. Ironically, most of these men represented jurisdictions that were added to those subject to the Voting Rights Act in 1975—ostensibly because these jurisdictions limited the opportunities of Hispanics to vote or to elect representatives of their own ethnic group.

Hundreds of Mexican Americans held local office as well. One study cites seven hundred Mexican American local officials in 1971 in Texas alone; and in twelve of the thirteen Texas counties with the largest Mexican American concentrations, the county commissions were controlled by Mexican Americans.[13] Says Thernstrom, "This situation was in glaring contrast with the Deep South prior to the Voting Rights Act, where the existence of large black populations had not forced white racists to share power with blacks. In fact, it was precisely in the areas of greatest black concentration that white supremacy thrived most."[14] No mention of these facts was made during the hearings.

Mexican Americans in Texas did face some harassment in voting, but those problems were not nearly universal. One lobbyist admitted to Thernstrom in a confidential interview, "What we found, we portrayed . . . as a giant, statewide pattern, which it really wasn't."[15] Witnesses cited incidents of abuses from a handful of Texas counties (out of 254 in the state), most notably Frio, Uvalde, and La Salle. Witnesses

charged that Mexican Americans did not receive bilingual assistance at the polls, that Mexican American voters were given
misinformation on po!¹ing places and voting procedures, that
Mexican American voters were harassed at the polls, and that
Mexican American poll watchers suffered similar treatment.[16]
These abuses, while serious, did not constitute the same kind
of denial of the right to vote that had provoked Congress in
1965 to usurp the right of southern states to make and enforce their own election laws. Nonetheless, Congress went
ahead to extend the burdensome strictures of the Voting
Rights Act to jurisdictions in which Mexican Americans and
other Hispanics lived. More than 375 jurisdictions were added
to those already covered under the act's special provisions.

THE NEW ENTITLEMENTS

The decision to grant Hispanics the same extraordinary protections southern black voters had been given did not occur
in a public policy vacuum. Between the mid-1960s and the
mid-1970s, a dramatic shift on the meaning of discrimination
took place. Indeed, this shift in definitions made it possible
for MALDEF and other Hispanic organizations to claim, on
the basis of quite shallow evidence, that Mexican Americans
and other Hispanics were systematically being denied the
right to vote. The civil rights legislation of the 1960s was based
on the principle that race, color, sex, national origin, or religion should not be an impediment to the enjoyment of rights
granted to all persons in this society. The premise underlying
all of the laws passed during the 1960s to protect civil rights
was that the rules that applied to one group—namely,
whites—should apply to all other groups, whether in employment, education, housing, or voting.

By 1975 the civil rights movement had changed its goals.
It was no longer content to have the same rules apply to whites

and blacks, men and women. Rather, it now urged that the rules themselves be changed so that minorities and women could compete under separate standards, provided that the results obtained improved the status of these groups. In other words, as long as more minorities and women were admitted to universities, were hired and promoted, and had their earnings go up relative to those of white males, disparate treatment of minorities and women was not only tolerated but encouraged. In the mid-1960s, the byword was *equal opportunity*; by 1975, it was *equal results*. Ultimately, results could be "equal" only if they were proportional. Everything was seen in terms of the group's right to its share of the pie. A "fair share" came to mean one equal to the group's proportion of the population. This definition applied whether one was talking about the distribution of jobs, the racial composition of schools and neighborhoods, or the voting rates of minorities. If minorities did not vote in the same proportion as nonminorities, discrimination was presumed to be the cause. Moreover, by 1975 the right to vote was being equated with the right to elect minority candidates. The voting *process* was no longer the focus; the voting *outcome* was.

Given this context, it is not surprising that Congress declared Hispanics the victims of voting discrimination. It was not essential to show that Hispanics were being kept from casting their votes because of their ethnicity. All that Hispanic organizations really needed to demonstrate was that proportionally fewer Hispanics voted and fewer Hispanic candidates were elected than non-Hispanic whites. (That fewer Mexican Americans were eligible to vote because far fewer of them were citizens apparently made no difference.) MALDEF's argument that Mexican Americans were underrepresented was sufficient rationale for Congress to transform the way elections could be conducted in more than 375 jurisdictions in the nation. MALDEF's victory extended the extraordinary protections of the Voting Rights Act to non-Hispanic groups as well: to Asians, American Indians, and Alaskan natives. Because of MALDEF's efforts, these specific groups became entitled to ballots in their own languages (though other non-English-speaking groups were not given this right). And the jurisdictions in which members of these groups lived became subject to extensive monitoring of their electoral processes.

NATIONWIDE APPLICATION

The 1975 Voting Rights Act amendments extended the special provisions of the act for seven more years. In 1965 Congress had enacted those provisions with the promise that—though extraordinarily tough—they would be temporary. By the time Congress considered the act again, in 1982, the "temporary" provisions had been in effect nearly twenty years, even though the kind of egregious denial of the right to vote they were meant to correct had long since disappeared. But the 1982 amendments to the Voting Rights Act went beyond extending the special provisions for ten more years. These amendments fundamentally changed the meaning of voting discrimination under the act and extended protection to minorities under this new definition to all political jurisdictions, not just those with literacy tests and low voter turnout.

The amendments of 1982 established a new definition of voting discrimination—namely, any practice that "results in a denial or abridgement of the right to vote." As was noted earlier, however, this "right to vote" had been interpreted by the courts to mean the right to elect members of one's own racial or ethnic group, although this principle had been applied only to jurisdictions covered by the preclearance provision. Under the 1982 amendments this standard became part of the act that applied to all states and political jurisdictions. The only way for a jurisdiction to prove that its voting procedures were nondiscriminatory would be to show "the extent to which members of a protected class have been elected to office in the state or political subdivision."[17] The practical effect of the 1982 amendments was to make it possible for minority groups to challenge virtually any practice that might result in fewer minorities being elected to office, especially in at-large voting and multimember districts. Black and Hispanic civil rights groups—long critical of at-large voting and multimember districts—would now be able to challenge these practices everywhere in the country.

When Congress considered the 1982 Voting Rights Act amendments, MALDEF once again led the Hispanic charge. The act had been an important tool in several lawsuits filed since 1975. Moreover, Hispanic witnesses claimed that the bilingual ballot provisions had enhanced the participation of Hispanic voters. One witness summarized the changes brought by bilingual ballots, quoting from a newspaper article from McAllen, Texas,

Dominga Sausedo was nervous as she walked from the cramped house to the neighborhood school a few blocks away. For the first time in the forty-eight years since she was born here in Texas, Mrs. Sausedo was on her way to vote. Like thousands of American citizens, Mrs. Sausedo speaks no English. The language and information barriers that existed until recently were enough to keep her away from the voting booth.[18]

Only Congressman Henry Hyde (R-Ill.) sounded a sour note during House hearings. "Is it common that someone would be born in America and live 48 years here and not be able to speak English or to understand it?" Hyde asked. "It is. It sure is," the witness responded, but offered no evidence to back up his claim.[19] (In fact, the overwhelming majority of Mexican American adults speak English; non-English-speaking Hispanics are mostly immigrants. Moreover, in order to become a naturalized citizen—and therefore eligible to vote—an immigrant must demonstrate a knowledge of English, unless he is older than fifty.) When Hyde pressed the point, arguing that more bilingual services "perpetuate or deny the incentive to learn English," he was told that bilingual education would eventually solve the problem of native-born Mexican Americans who could not understand English well enough to cast a ballot in that language. Not even Congressman Hyde seemed willing to ask the witness how instructing Hispanic children in Spanish was going to enable more of them to cast ballots in English in future generations.[20]

THE SEARCH FOR SAFE HISPANIC SEATS

Hispanic organizations cite the changes in the Voting Rights Act as a major factor in the growth of Hispanic political power, but the real winners may be Hispanic political operatives, not Hispanics themselves. In its twentieth-anniversary report, issued in 1988, MALDEF credits the Voting Rights Act with its victory in a series of suits it filed to end at-large voting and multimember districts in Texas, New Mexico, and elsewhere. MALDEF claims it was "actively involved in redrawing election districts at the local level based on the 1980 Census," citing a major victory in a Chicago redistricting case that led to the court-ordered creation of four Hispanic wards "which changed the political future of Chicago."[21] In 1985 the U.S. Department of Justice filed suit in a redistricting plan for the Los Angeles City Council, which forced the city to create a heavily Hispanic district from which a Mexican American was eventually elected. A similar suit in 1988 against Los Angeles County also charged that Hispanics were being denied the right to elect a Hispanic member of the Los Angeles County Board of Supervisors.

Indeed, more Hispanic seats have been created because of the Voting Rights Act and more Hispanics have been elected to office from such districts. This pattern will very likely increase when state legislatures complete redistricting plans in 1991, following the last decennial census, which will record a huge increase in the number of Hispanics living in the United States. But the growing number of Hispanic electoral districts is not necessarily an indication of greater political participation on the part of Hispanics—at least not as measured in actual voting. At the national level, a smaller percentage of them voted in 1988 than in 1976. A smaller percentage of them were eligible to vote in 1988 because a smaller proportion were citizens, however, as a result of rising immigration levels and low naturalization rates (a subject treated at greater length in chapter 6). Yet, Hispanic leaders cite low voting rates as proof of discrimination, even though such figures are based on population numbers that include a large percentage of noncitizens ineligible to vote. This "discrimination," in turn, justifies creating safe Hispanic seats.

The manipulation of immigration data to create Hispanic electoral seats continues to provoke controversy, especially when it involves illegal aliens. Legislative seats are apportioned on the basis of population figures determined by the Census Bureau, which counts citizens and noncitizens alike. States with large numbers of immigrants and illegal aliens, like California, benefit from this practice at the expense of states with few immigrants. For example, since the 435 seats in the House of Representatives are apportioned among the states according to population, those states that have experienced population growth will gain congressional seats through reapportionment. Recently, some states slated to lose seats in the 1991 reapportionment sued, charging that illegal aliens should not be counted to apportion legislative districts; but the Supreme Court upheld the practice.[22] Nonetheless, many people find it objectionable that the growing Hispanic political clout is based at least partly on the granting of representation to people who have no legal right to be here.

The practice has other consequences as well. The political

scientist Peter Skerry warns that using illegal aliens to create safe minority voting districts will result in "rotten boroughs, with large and growing numbers of 'constituents' unable to vote." Politicians who represent these districts can act with impunity even when their actions are clearly detrimental to the interests of their non–enfranchised constituents. What's more, Skerry maintains, "the officeholders who represent such districts are more likely to be responsive to the politicians who designed them than to the people who live in them."[23]

Efforts to create safe Hispanic districts in California illustrate Skerry's point. In one recent election, for example, only 28 people cast ballots in one Hispanic precinct, compared with an average of 146 votes in Anglo precincts in the same election.[24] The precinct was located in a district created specifically to give Hispanics a safe city council seat, one in which Hispanics constitute the majority of eligible voters, following a successful 1985 suit brought by the U.S. Justice Department under the Voting Rights Act. Gloria Molina was elected in 1986 to represent the new district. Like most efforts to redraw district lines to create safe Hispanic seats, this one used population figures rather than figures based on the number of citizens able to vote. Consequently, the district comprises about 200,000 residents—the same number as non-Hispanic districts—but the number of registered voters in the district in 1989 was only about 38,000, compared with about 118,000 in a similar Anglo district.[25] The discrepancy in registration is due largely to the presence in Molina's district of so many immigrants, about half of whom are illegal aliens. The effect, as Skerry notes, is to concentrate power in a handful of Hispanic elected officials who represent districts consisting of relatively few eligible voters.

The vote that Councilwoman Molina casts in the city council chambers is equal to that of council members who represent more than three times the number of eligible voters she does. Such wide variations in representation between legislative districts led to the Supreme Court's landmark ruling in *Baker* v. *Carr* (1962), establishing the principle of "one man, one vote," which became a rallying cry in the civil rights era. Ironically, some Hispanic civil rights organizations seem willing to abandon this principle if it means greater political power for a few Hispanic elected officials. Nor do such "rotten boroughs" necessarily advance the interests of Hispanics seeking political office, as another Los Angeles voting rights case illustrates.

In 1988 MALDEF (later joined by the Justice Department) filed a suit in federal court alleging that the Los Angeles County Board of Supervisors discriminated against Hispanic voters. Los Angeles County—the largest county in the nation, with 8.7 million residents—is governed by a five-member board of supervisors. Even though 33 percent of the population of Los Angeles County is Hispanic, no Hispanic had been elected to the board. After a long trial in which Hispanic organizations testified that the failure to elect a Hispanic to the board since 1875 constituted proof of discrimination, a federal court found that the board of supervisors had discriminated in drawing election district lines and ordered parties in the suit to submit new plans that would redress Hispanic grievances. In an ironic twist, one day after the court declared that no Hispanic could be elected without creating a new, "safe" district, a Hispanic woman was the top vote-getter for a vacant seat on the board in an election in which the old, supposedly discriminatory district lines were used. The election results were voided when the Ninth Circuit Court of Appeals upheld the lower-court decision and ordered a new election. The appeals court also accepted a redistricting plan drawn up by MALDEF, which was so badly gerrymandered that the *Wall Street Journal* described it as a "poodle-shaped district ... [which] packs in as many Hispanic Democrats as possible." One Hispanic whose residence was left out of the new district was Sarah Flores, the Hispanic Republican who had placed first in the earlier election. Although the court ruled that Flores could still run in the new district even though she did not live within the new lines, her base of support had been eroded.

In a four-way race in January 1991, which included Councilwoman Molina and a Democratic state senator, Art Torres, Flores came in third. Molina and Torres competed in a runoff election the following month, which Molina won with 55 percent of the vote. Voter turnout was light, however; only 23 percent of those registered voted, but even this figure underestimates how few persons actually participated in the election. The new district is made up of a population of about 975,000 persons of voting age, but fewer than 83,000 persons voted. No doubt, participation was so low because many who live in the district are not U.S. citizens. Nonetheless, it is difficult to understand how Hispanic leaders could herald the election as a major victory in the fight for Hispanic political participation when fewer than one in ten adults even voted.

WINNERS OR LOSERS?

The extension of the Voting Rights Act to Hispanic voters produced certain trade-offs. Like other ethnic entitlements, such as affirmative action, voting rights protection grants certain benefits but at the expense of accepting what could become a self-fulfilling prophecy—namely, that Hispanics will be permanently disadvantaged. The act treats Hispanics like current and future victims of widespread, persistent, and systemic discrimination in the political arena, despite evidence to the contrary. Six Hispanics have been elected governor in three states in this century, even though Hispanics do not constitute anything like a majority of voters in any state. In Florida, where Bob Martinez was elected governor in 1986, Hispanics—mostly Cubans—made up only 11 percent of the population, less than one-third of whom voted in the election.[26] Clearly, these Hispanic candidates were elected because a majority of the voters believed their political qualifications, not their ethnicity, to be relevant. Even in places where Hispanics make up a large portion of the population, factors other than discrimination may explain why no Hispanics hold office. In Los Angeles County, for example, a Hispanic had run for the board of supervisors only once prior to 1990, in 1959, when Edward Roybal (now a member of the U.S. House of Representatives) lost the election in a runoff. The Voting Rights Act notwithstanding, it is still not possible to elect a Hispanic if Hispanic candidates do not run. Nor does it suffice to say that Hispanic candidates will be discouraged from running unless they can be guaranteed districts in which Hispanics constitute a majority of voters. That obviously didn't stop the Hispanics who were elected governor of their state; nor did it discourage me from running for (and winning) the Republican nomination for the U.S. Senate seat from Maryland, though Hispanics make up less than 1 percent of the voters in the state.

The notion of "proportional representation" that undergirds arguments in most voting rights cases is fraught with potential dangers. If Hispanics are *entitled* to Hispanic elected officials in areas where their proportion of the population is high, what about areas in which it is low? The natural corollary to the notion that Hispanics can best represent the interests of Hispanics is that non-Hispanics can best represent the interests of non-Hispanics. This is a dangerous game for any minority to play. Historically, quotas have been used as a ceiling to minority achievement, not a floor, as Jews and, more recently, Asians discovered. Strict proportional representation would bar the election of Hispanic governors, senators, presidents in return for the guarantee of some city council members, supervisors, school board members, and assorted other local officials from Hispanic districts. When confronted with the plea to create safe Hispanic seats during the Voting Rights Act hearings in 1982, Congressman Henry Hyde responded, "Well maybe someone who isn't a Mexican American can be an honest, decent person and do a good job in office...."[27] Hyde's formula at least offers the possibility that Hispanics, too, are capable of representing the interests of non-Hispanics, that Hispanic political leaders can become more than power brokers for their ethnic constituency.

The danger in buying into the notion of safe Hispanic districts is not just that it will limit the aspirations of those Hispanics who want to run for public office. More vital issues are at stake. The success of this voting rights strategy depends on dissuading Hispanics from integrating into the larger community. But this runs counter to the choices Hispanics are already freely making. As the demographer Douglas Massey points out, Hispanics are not highly segregated even in areas with large Hispanic populations, including Los Angeles, San Antonio, and Miami. "Indeed," says Massey, "a lack of high segregation on any dimension is the most common pattern for Hispanics...."[28] The political scientist Bruce Cain also reports that Hispanics who improve their economic status and move to more affluent neighborhoods are more likely to switch their political affiliation from Democratic to Republican.[29] Are Hispanic leaders prepared to argue that it is in Hispanics' interest to remain congregated in inner-city barrios in order to enlarge the roster of Hispanic (and Democratic) elected officials? Those barrios now are occupied increasingly by new immigrants, many of them illegal.

If middle-class Hispanics continue to choose to leave Hispanic neighborhoods, Hispanic organizations will be forced to rely even more heavily on noncitizens to demonstrate large concentrations of "underrepresented" Hispanic "voters." This, too, will have unfortunate consequences, devaluing the rewards of American citizenship. What incentive will there be for Hispanic politicians to encourage Latino immigrants to become citizens if the mere presence of immigrants in a district ensures the election of a Hispanic candidate? Latin immigrants, especially Mexicans, already have abysmally low naturalization rates (see chapter 6), and the cynical manipulation of immigrant population data to increase Hispanic political power will not make matters better.

The history of Hispanic involvement with the Voting Rights Act is a clear example of short-term gains purchased at the expense of long-range achievement. Hispanic leaders were quite successful in convincing legislators and the courts that Hispanics were politically powerless without the intervention of the federal government. But in order to keep federal protection, Hispanics must continue to fail. If Hispanics move beyond the confines of inner-city barrios into middle-class suburbs, as they are already doing, will federal courts persist in creating gerrymandered districts that scoop up scattered Hispanic voters in a broad geographical area as the court did in Los Angeles County? And will Hispanics who have achieved middle-class status want to have their political fate linked to that of impoverished immigrants? At least one Hispanic activist suggests that is exactly the point of the effort in Los Angeles County: "It ties the fortunes of the Latino middle class to those of lower-income Latinos. The Latino middle class, the chief beneficiary of the civil rights movement, can no longer cold-shoulder the interests of the Latino poor without paying a political price, because the two now constitute one political community."[30] This is an odd reversal of the traditional ethnic model in the United States. Instead of encouraging those at the bottom to climb higher, it pulls down those who have already risen. There will be no winners if Hispanics accept this strategy.

CHAPTER 3

The Power Brokers

In large part, the success of Hispanics in securing bilingual education programs and safe seats for Hispanic candidates testifies to their political power. The doubling of the size of the Hispanic population over the last twenty years has led politicians and policy makers to listen attentively when Hispanic leaders speak. They assume, after all, that these leaders speak for twenty million people. And for the past two decades, Hispanic leaders have convinced politicians and policy makers that Hispanics want and deserve special treatment—everything from bilingual education for Spanish-speaking children to protected status at the polls for Latino adults—and that they require protection from an alien, Anglo society in which they cannot compete. In doing so, these leaders have enhanced their own power, but their methods jeopardize the future integration of Hispanics into this society.

Contemporary Hispanic politics owes much to the civil rights movement. Hispanic political leaders were trained in civil rights organizations in the 1960s and 1970s, and they adopted their strategy from the movement's political battles. Today, Hispanic organizations seek to advance Hispanic interests by demanding entitlements based on ethnicity and disadvantaged status. But in order to remain eligible for such

entitlements, Hispanics must continue to be outside the social, political, and economic mainstream. The fight for political recognition for Hispanics is no longer a fight to be
included but rather one to be treated like a separate, special
group, subject to rules and standards different from those
that apply to the general population. When did Hispanic
leaders give up the fight to help Hispanics join the mainstream? And how did that transformation take place?

IN THE BEGINNING

Before the affirmative action age, there were no *Hispanics*,
only Mexicans, Puerto Ricans, Cubans, and so on. Indeed, few
efforts were made to forge an alliance among the various Hispanic subgroups until the 1970s, when competition with
blacks for college admissions, jobs, and other rewards of affirmative action made it advantageous for Hispanics to join
forces in order to demand a larger share of the pie. In addition to having no common history, these groups were more
or less geographically isolated from one another. Mexican
Americans lived in the Southwest, Puerto Ricans in the Northeast, mostly in New York, and Cubans in Florida; smaller enclaves were to be found in New Jersey and elsewhere. For
many years Puerto Ricans and Cubans focused more on politics in their homeland than on domestic U.S. politics. Puerto
Ricans continue to be concerned about the status of Puerto
Rico, whether it will remain a commonwealth, politically and
economically linked to the United States, become a state, or
gain independence. Cubans, too, remain concerned with the
fate of their island, especially in the wake of the retreat from
communism throughout the world. Some Cuban exiles have
formed a government-in-waiting, in the hopes that Fidel Castro's regime will soon come to an end. But Puerto Ricans and
Cubans have both become actively involved in U.S. politics as

well. Puerto Ricans and Cuban Americans together hold only about 250 elected offices in the United States out of a total of more than 4,000 held by all Hispanics.[1] And both groups have joined Mexican Americans as major beneficiaries of the politics of affirmative action, even though Cuban Americans are hardly a disadvantaged group by any measure.

The most important political organizations—and the oldest—exist in the Mexican American community. Mexican Americans make up two-thirds of the entire Hispanic population, some 13.3 million persons, and are the most widely dispersed of any of the Hispanic groups, with large Mexican-origin populations in the Midwest as well as the West and the Southwest. The Mexican-origin population is more than six times as large as the next-largest group, Puerto Ricans, and wields the greatest influence on public policy toward Hispanics as a result. Mexican American organizations have existed for nearly a hundred years, and the earliest groups very much fit the traditional immigrant model. Like their counterparts among other immigrant groups, they were formed to provide mutual assistance in the form of death benefits and care for the needy and to help their members adjust to life in an often hostile environment.

As early as 1894 a mutual-aid society of Mexicans was formed in the Southwest, and hundreds of such organizations appeared in the next few decades. In his study of Mexican American political organization, Ralph Guzman notes that "these groups, while performing a limited welfare role, were, in large part, substitutes for external Anglo organizations which Mexican Americans could not easily join."[2] Not surprisingly, middle-class and wealthy Mexican nationals and Mexican Americans made up the bulk of the membership of such organizations. Excluded by ethnic prejudice from participating fully in the civic life of their communities, they created their own business and civic groups, which often mirrored those of the larger community. Mexican Americans joined such organizations not because they wished to remain separate from the majority culture but because they were frequently kept outside it.

Puerto Ricans also established mutual-aid societies in New York as early as 1918; but the Puerto Rican population at the time was quite small, about seven thousand people. When Cubans migrated in the 1960s, the pattern of assistance to immigrants and refugees had already changed dramatically, with the government taking over many of the functions of resettlement, especially bearing the costs of financial assistance to refugees.[3] Today various community groups assist new arrivals from Central and South America, but most of these groups are supported with funds from outside the community, either through private philanthropic foundations and corporations or through government grants.

Most of the early Hispanic organizations promoted assimilation and integration; indeed, their struggle was to have Hispanics accepted as fully participating members of American society. The people who joined organizations like the League of United Latin American Citizens (LULAC), the oldest Hispanic organization among those still active today, did so because they wanted to promote greater integration of Hispanics into the majority culture. LULAC was formed in Texas in 1929 from the union of several smaller Hispanic groups. Its emphasis was strictly assimilationist. Only U.S. citizens could become LULAC members, and Spanish was not used in the official proceedings of the organization. In its declaration of aims and purposes (which remains unchanged to this day), the organization lists among the duties of LULAC members the following:

To foster the acquisition and facile use of the official language of our country [sic] that we may thereby equip ourselves and our families for the fullest enjoyment of our rights and privileges and the efficient discharge of our duties and obligations to this, our country.[4]

Other Hispanic organizations, especially in the Mexican American community, also emphasized patriotism and integration into American life. Indeed, the second-oldest major Hispanic organization, the American G.I. Forum, began as a veterans' group to promote recognition of the military contribution of Mexican Americans. The organization was founded by Hector Garcia, a surgeon from Corpus Christi, Texas, shortly after World War II. Dr. Garcia organized his fellow Mexican American veterans when a mortuary in Three Rivers, Texas, in 1948 refused to handle the funeral of a local Mexican American who had been killed in the battle for the Philippines and whose body had finally been returned for burial. The incident sparked the intervention of Lyndon B. Johnson, then senator, whose intercession won the right of the soldier, Felix Longoria, to be buried at Arlington National Cemetery.

The Second World War marked a turning point for Hispanic activism. Hispanics served with great distinction in the war, earning more Congressional Medals of Honor per capita than any other group. Moreover, unlike blacks, Hispanics served in integrated military units, which brought them into contact with other Americans and introduced them, for the first time, to Americans who lived outside the Southwest. More than 100,000 Puerto Ricans served in the military during the war; later, many of these men and their families decided to migrate from the island in search of greater economic opportunity in the United States. Hispanics returned from the war expecting better treatment than was the standard fare for Mexican Americans and Puerto Ricans in most places. Hispanics wanted to increase their earnings and social standing, live where they wanted, and send their children to better schools. Indeed, there was significant upward mobility for Mexican Americans in this period, especially in California and other areas outside Texas, and for Puerto Ricans who migrated to New York City. For all the relative gains in their social and economic status, Hispanics still lagged significantly behind non-Hispanic whites, and they continued to face some discrimination in employment and housing. During this period, groups such as LULAC, the American G.I. Forum, and ASPIRA (a Puerto Rican group involved in education in New York) fought for the full integration of Hispanics into American society, often taking their fight against discrimination into court, filing suits against de facto segregation in schools, for example.

These groups comprised middle-class and aspiring middle-class Hispanics. The assimilationist politics of the early Mexican American organizations was based on the members' belief that Mexican Americans should participate fully in the society in which they lived. Efforts to keep Hispanics apart from the majority population and its institutions were viewed as hostile to Hispanics and discriminatory. These early organizations often acted as pressure groups, urging elected officials to correct abuses, whether to eliminate discriminatory treatment or to provide better public services to Hispanics. For the most part, though, the organizations themselves did not get involved directly in partisan politics. (Hispanics were, in fact, active in partisan politics in Texas, New Mexico, and elsewhere, but by way of the party structures in those states, not separate Mexican American organizations.) After the postwar decade, however, two developments changed the direction of Hispanic activism: the civil rights movement and the "discovery" of Hispanics by philanthropic foundations. The Industrial Areas Foundation (IAF), started in the 1940s in Chicago by the community organizer Saul Alinsky, was among the first groups from outside the Hispanic community to become involved in the barrios of the Southwest.

The IAF helped found the Community Service Organization (CSO) in Los Angeles in 1947. Like other Alinsky groups around the country, the CSO promoted social activism and political participation among blacks and other minorities.

Whereas LULAC and the G.I. Forum had been indigenous Mexican American organizations, the CSO included signifi- cant numbers of non-Hispanics in its leadership and received funding from the IAF and local unions. The CSO printed and distributed bilingual materials on how to get sidewalks and curbs installed in Mexican American neighborhoods, and it promoted social action on issues such as housing discrimi- nation and police brutality. But perhaps its most important work was in the political arena. According to the historian Ralph Guzman, the CSO registered more than 32,000 new Mexican American voters in Los Angeles County in 1950 through the efforts of more than a hundred deputy registrars who were CSO volunteers, many of them students, house- wives, or unemployed workers, who canvassed Latino neigh- borhoods. In the 1950 election the CSO's first chairman, Edward Roybal, was elected to the Los Angeles City Council. (Roybal also ran for lieutenant governor of California in 1954, outpolling the Democratic candidate for governor, though both lost, and ran unsuccessfully for the Los Angeles County Board of Supervisors in 1959; he was elected in 1962 to the U.S. House of Representatives, where he still serves.) Ironically, Roybal's departure from the CSO led to a vacuum of leadership that may have contributed to the organization's later decline in influence. Although the CSO continues its work in Los Angeles and elsewhere in California, the orga- nization is now mostly a social services agency.

SEPARATISM AND THE RISE OF RADICAL POLITICS

The 1950s and early 1960s were relatively quiet years in terms of Hispanic activism. The one notable exception occurred in the Puerto Rican community, where the rise of a radical in- dependence movement in Puerto Rico spilled over onto the

mainland. In 1950 Puerto Rican extremists attempted to as-
sassinate President Harry Truman when he was leaving Blair
House, a temporary residence across the street from the White
House, where he was living while repairs were done on the
White House. In 1954 Puerto Rican terrorists opened fire in
the House of Representatives, injuring five members of Congress. By and large, however, Hispanic activism was muted
during this time, and what activity there was took place in
the electoral arena. Throughout the early 1960s Hispanics
made gains in electing Hispanics at all levels of government.
In 1950 there were only twenty Mexican American state legislators in the Southwest, all in New Mexico; by 1965 there
were thirty-five in four states.[5] In addition to Edward Roybal
in California, two Mexican Americans were elected congressmen in Texas, Henry B. Gonzalez and Kika de la Garza; and
Puerto Rican city councilmen and state legislators were
elected in New York. Hispanics were beginning to make gains
within the system at the very time that some Hispanic leaders
proposed that the system itself should be overturned.

In part, this shift was simply a symptom of the times, for it
occurred at the height of the black power and antiwar move-
ments sweeping the country. The spillover into the Mexican
American and Puerto Rican communities was predictable, especially among the predominantly (though not exclusively)
college-educated young men who led many of the more radical Hispanic groups of the era. Four Mexican American
groups achieved particular prominence during this period:
the Mexican American Political Association (MAPA), the Alianza Federal de Mercedes, the Crusade for Justice, and La
Raza Unida party. Though each group was organized in a
different state, at separate times, and under different leadership, all shared a profound distrust of non-Hispanics and majority institutions. According to the leaders of these groups,
Anglo society would never accept Mexican Americans as full
and equal participants, no matter how hard Mexican Ameri-

cans tried to conform to the values of the majority culture. Therefore, they argued, Mexican Americans must separate themselves from the majority society. What was perhaps surprising about such views was that they came at the very time that discrimination against Mexican Americans was diminishing and Mexican Americans were making impressive gains in their economic and educational status.

The Mexican American Political Association (MAPA) was founded in 1959 by two political activists frustrated with the lack of Latino influence in California Democratic party politics, Bert Corona and Edward Quevedo. MAPA became the dominant Hispanic political organization through the mid-1970s, especially in California.[6] At the height of its influence, it claimed more than sixty chapters in several southwestern states. Non-Hispanics were excluded from participation, because the leaders of MAPA clearly believed that only Mexican Americans could adequately represent the interests of other Mexican Americans. This belief carried over from the internal politics of the organization to electoral politics. The organization worked to elect Mexican American candidates, not just candidates of any ethnic origin who were sympathetic to the interests of a Latino constituency. Increasingly, leaders of the organization came to believe that Mexican American candidates would have to steer their own, separate course, unable to rely on help from either political party. As Ralph Guzman has reported, "MAPA announced that it did not expect help from the 'vultures' in the Republican Party but that it was also aware that 'some friends in the Democratic Party and some bosses in the labor movement have deserted us.' "[7]

In 1961 MAPA led an unsuccessful effort to incorporate East Los Angeles as a separate political entity. The expanse east of the city of Los Angeles is a largely Mexican American residential and commercial area, which was (and remains) the largest unincorporated community in the country. In Guzman's words,

MAPA stressed the need to educate the Mexican American working class. Leaders argued that the drive to incorporate [East Los Angeles] ... would surely fail if the citizens did not understand what they had in common with each other and how incorporation would benefit each household.... Corona and other MAPA members stressed that East Los Angeles was predominantly Mexican American and that it should be controlled by Mexican Americans.[8]

Although MAPA failed to win support for a separate corporate jurisdiction in East Los Angeles, its effort was a precursor to the drive a decade later by MALDEF and other Hispanic groups to create the separate Mexican American political jurisdictions discussed in the preceding chapter.

MAPA in California and, later, La Raza Unida party in Texas (examined below) both used electoral politics to pursue a separatist strategy on behalf of Mexican Americans. A different approach was taken by two groups that appeared in New Mexico and Colorado and preached a kind of secessionism. The first, Alianza Federal de Mercedes, actually attempted an armed takeover of government lands on behalf of Spanish land-grant holders in northern New Mexico. The second, the Crusade for Justice, proclaimed its irredentist allegiance to a mythical Mexican empire, Aztlán. Like many radical groups of the era, the Alianza and the Crusade for Justice enjoyed short but subtly influential reigns. They promoted the idea that Mexican Americans in the Southwest were not merely disadvantaged members of this society but, rather, a conquered people.

In many ways, the appearance of a radical group like the Alianza in New Mexico was surprising. New Mexico's Hispanic population had traditionally been quite powerful politically and successful by most standards. Alone among the territories acquired in the war with Mexico, New Mexico had a sizable population in 1848—roughly sixty thousand persons. Much of the Hispanic population of present-day New

Mexico is descended from early Spanish colonists who settled northern New Mexico in the seventeenth and eighteenth centuries. To this day, many New Mexicans prefer to be called Spanish American or Hispano and eschew identification with Mexico.[9] Indeed, New Mexico was governed by the republic of Mexico (after Mexico won its independence from Spain in 1821) for only twenty-five years of its nearly four-hundred-year history.

More important, however, the indigenous Hispanic population of New Mexico has played an important role in every aspect of the state's life since New Mexico's admission to the Union, in 1912. The state has elected four Hispanic governors (the first in 1917 and the most recent in 1983); three Hispanic U.S. senators (one of whom, Dennis Chavez, served for twenty-seven years and became the powerful head of the Senate Public Works Committee); seven members of Congress; and a succession of Hispanic state representatives (both the original speaker of the state house and the president pro tempore of the state senate were Hispanos, as were eight others who have served in those positions to the present); as well as scores of local officials in the past eighty years.[10] Prejudice of the kind encountered by Mexican Americans in Texas, for example, was rarely a problem for New Mexico's Hispanos. As a 1954 study of Spanish Americans noted, "The Hispano of New Mexico may go to any school, be served at any cafe, stay at any hotel, ride anywhere in the streetcars or get a haircut at any barbershop."[11] In addition, Hispanos were represented among all social classes in the state.

Despite the relative openness of New Mexican society, however, many Hispanos lived in poverty at the time the Alianza was formed, in 1966, especially in the rural farming villages in the northern part of the state. Reies Lopez Tijerina, an itinerant Pentecostal preacher from Texas who founded the Alianza, was able to exploit the resentment that some New Mexico Hispanos felt regarding what they considered to be their dispossession from the land. Indeed, over a million acres of land—nearly half the area of New Mexico—is either Indian reservation or is owned by the federal or state government. Much of it is in regions formerly consisting of lands the king of Spain granted to New Mexico families and their descendants.

In 1966 Tijerina and some 350 followers attempted to take over a portion of the Kit Carson National Forest. Tijerina was sentenced to two years in prison for this first Alianza assault, in which two forest rangers were taken hostage, but it was a second raid, while he was out on bail on this conviction, that brought him national attention. On June 5, 1967, twenty Alianza members seized the courthouse in Tierra Amarilla, New Mexico. A state patrolman and a deputy sheriff (both Hispanos) were shot, two persons were taken hostage, and the Alianza band fled into the hills. Tijerina and his followers surrendered a few days later, after a massive manhunt. Tijerina was brought to trial on fifty-four criminal counts but was acquitted in his first trial. The prosecution's initial case was hurt when the chief prosecution witness was murdered before the case came to trial. Tijerina was subsequently tried and convicted of assault and destruction of federal property. For his combined convictions, he served a little more than two years in federal prison.

Tijerina's Alianza never became a mass movement. At the height of its notoriety, it had no more than 3,000 members.[12] Nonetheless, the theme that the Alianza struck—that the land forming the American Southwest had been wrongfully wrested from Mexico and from the indigenous Mexican population—became the rallying cry for many Mexican Americans in the new radical movement.

Among the proponents of this new *movimiento* was Rodolfo ("Corky") Gonzales, who established the Crusade for Justice in Denver, Colorado, in the mid-1960s. Gonzales, who grew up in a lower-class Mexican American neighborhood in Denver and was a promising boxer in his youth, became a successful bail bondsman and Democratic party activist before he decided to abandon establishment politics and found his own organization. In 1969 the Crusade for Justice hosted the Youth Liberation Conference in Denver, which was attended by more than fifteen hundred. The outcome of the conference was a manifesto that proclaimed a separate nation for Hispanics, now dubbed Chicanos, after a slang term popular among lower-class Mexican American youth gangs, known as *pachucos*, in the 1940s. Calling their nation Aztlán, after the mythical territory north of modern Mexico from which the Aztecs were supposed to have migrated in the eleventh century, these young Mexican American activists declared that Chicanos would reclaim the land taken from their forefathers by the "brutal 'gringo' invasion of our territories." Their Plan Espiritual de Aztlán became the focal point for a generation of Mexican American activists:

Aztlan belongs to those who plant the seeds, water the fields, and gather the crops and not to the foreign Europeans. We do not recognize capricious frontiers on the Bronze Continent.... Before the world, before all of North America, before all our brothers in the Bronze Continent, we are a nation. We are a union of free *pueblos*. We are *Aztlan*. *Por la raza todo, fuera de la raza nada* [Everything for the race, nothing outside the race].[13]

Whereas Tijerina had protested that the Hispanos of New Mexico had been robbed of land granted them by the king of Spain, Gonzales's followers were asserting a different claim to the land, one that predated the appearance of the "foreign Europeans," including the Spaniards. By asserting the myth of Aztlán, these Chicano activists were disavowing their European roots. (The reality that the culture of Mexico, from which many of their parents and grandparents had come, was profoundly influenced by its Spanish as well as its Indian heritage was conveniently ignored.) Chicano nationalism be-came the driving force among much of the politically active Hispanic population of the Southwest in the late 1960s and early 1970s.

Although both Tijerina's Alianza and Gonzales's Crusade for Justice remained radical-fringe organizations, the move-ment toward ethnic separatism grew in importance in the early 1970s. Mexican American student groups, which adopted a militant nationalist stance, sprang up on college campuses across the Southwest. Organizations like the Brown Berets of East Los Angeles imitated the ferocity of the Black Panthers, and bombings and political violence became a rare but powerful feature of radical Chicano politics. A similar phenomenon occurred in New York, where young Puerto Ri-cans organized the Young Lords and the Puerto Rican Revo-lutionary Workers Organization, both militant separatist groups that advocated, and sometimes engaged in, violence. But for the most part, the activities of the radical organiza-tions followed a path separate from (albeit occasionally par-allel to) that of mainstream Hispanic political organizations. Only in Texas, birthplace of La Raza Unida party, did the movement for Chicano nationalism inspire support in the mainstream Mexican American population.

The organizers of MAPA and of La Raza Unida party shared a distrust of the major political parties. MAPA leaders believed that the Democratic party was happy to have the votes of Mexican Americans but would refuse to give them leadership roles within the party itself; Republicans, in their eyes, were not even interested in vying for Mexican American votes. MAPA's solution was to field Mexican American can-didates within the Democratic party and to rally the Mexican American community to support only their fellow Chicanos. The organizers of La Raza Unida, on the other hand, consid-ered it insufficient to support Mexican American candidates if those men, once elected, became part of the political establishment, as they believed the Texas Democratic congressmen Henry B. Gonzalez (first elected in 1961) and Kika de la Garza (first elected in 1964) had. As one contemporary analyst described it, "La Raza Unida looked upon the Mexican American official or leader who replaced an Anglo but continued with the same values and traditions as merely an extension of the white power structure in a dark face."[14]

By 1970 La Raza Unida had gained sufficient support to field successful candidates in local elections in predominantly Mexican American southern Texas. La Raza Unida candidates gained control of the city council and board of education in Crystal City and were successful elsewhere in Cotulla and Carrizo Springs, Texas.[15] Spurred by their success in local elections, La Raza Unida activists decided to field a candidate for statewide office in 1972. Ramsey Muniz—a young lawyer who grew up in a poor, Spanish-speaking household and worked his way out of the Corpus Christi *barrio* on a college athletic scholarship to Baylor University—was the party's nominee for the governorship. Although Muniz was unsuccessful in his quest, he managed to win 214,118 votes, 6 percent of the popular vote statewide, depriving Dolph Briscoe, the Democratic party candidate, of a majority win. (Briscoe became the first Texas governor to be elected by a plurality.)[16]

La Raza Unida party's popularity was short-lived and never managed to extend beyond Texas, though unsuccessful attempts were made to run La Raza Unida candidates in Colorado and in California. Internal dissension contributed to the demise of La Raza Unida, but the party's major failing was its radical image. Much of the Mexican American establishment opposed the party. Indeed, Congressman Henry B. Gonzalez, the first Mexican American elected to Congress from Texas and a liberal Democrat, was a longtime nemesis of the party's founder, Jose Angel Gutierrez. At a press conference in 1969, Gutierrez was quoted as saying, "We have got to eliminate the gringo, and what I mean by that is if the worst comes to the worst, we have got to kill him."[17] At the time, Gutierrez was affiliated with the Mexican American Youth Organization (MAYO). Gonzalez became so enraged by Gutierrez's rhetoric that he took to the floor of the U.S. House of Representatives to accuse Gutierrez of promoting racial hatred. Gonzalez also attacked the Ford Foundation for financially supporting the organization through an indirect $10,000 grant to MAYO given by the Mexican American Unity Council of San Antonio, a Ford Foundation grantee. The Ford Foundation, fearing that the MAYO incident would strengthen congressional efforts already under way to limit political involvement by tax-exempt foundations, announced it would bar MAYO from receiving additional Ford Foundation money.[18]

By the mid-1970s it had became unfashionable in Mexican American circles to spout extremist separatist rhetoric. Mexican Americans found an increasingly warm reception in both of the major political parties, as mainstream politicians noted the rapidly growing size of the Mexican American population. Richard Nixon launched a highly publicized effort to attract Mexican Americans to his reelection effort in 1972 (which may have included clandestine payoffs to La Raza Unida activists in Texas—who, the Republicans rightly believed, siphoned votes from the Democratic party).[19] Nonetheless, the era of radical Mexican American politics left its mark. The idea that only Hispanics could represent Hispanics became political orthodoxy throughout the Hispanic leadership and ultimately gained acceptance in the larger Anglo political establishment.

For all its faults, the radical era in Mexican American politics did produce some genuine, though ephemeral, leaders. Bert Corona of MAPA, Corky Gonzales of the Crusade for Justice, and Jose Angel Gutierrez of La Raza Unida developed real followings within the Mexican American communities in which they were active. When these leaders and their groups were no longer able to command support in their communities, the leaders disappeared from the scene (or went back to establishment politics) and the organizations died out. Without the support from the Hispanic population—or even a small nucleus within it—these organizations could not sustain themselves. In that sense, they were responsive to the communities they represented. But the organizations that began to emerge as these radical groups declined developed their own independent base of support outside the Hispanic community—in the large, mainstream foundations. These new foundation-supported groups could afford to pursue their own agenda, without broad, popular support from the Hispanic community—and they did.

THE FOUNDATIONS AND
THE HISPANIC LEADERSHIP

The Ford Foundation was the first to become involved with Hispanics and remains the most extensively involved. Although the Ford Foundation is headquartered in New York City, its initial interest in the Hispanic community was not with the growing Puerto Rican population in the city but with Mexican Americans in the Southwest. In 1963 it provided the funding for a major study of Mexican Americans undertaken at UCLA. The Mexican-American Study Project spanned five years, included field research in twenty cities, and ultimately produced an authoritative work on the history, demography, institutions, and political participation of Mexican Americans, *The Mexican-American People: The Nation's Second Largest Minority*, by Leo Grebler, Joan Moore, and Ralph Guzman.[20]

In 1968 the Ford Foundation again commissioned a study of Hispanics—this time an internal document that would serve as a guide to the foundation's action. This study, too, focused on Mexican Americans, concluding that Mexican Americans were disorganized and fragmented and in need of a national organization to serve their social, economic, and political needs. On the basis of these findings, the foundation decided to help create two major Hispanic organizations: the Mexican American Legal Defense and Education Fund, patterned after the NAACP's Legal Defense Fund, and the Southwest Council of La Raza, which later became the National Council of La Raza. In the two decades since then, these organizations have become the most influential Hispanic public policy groups in the country.

What the Ford Foundation saw as disorganization and fragmentation in the Hispanic community may, in fact, have simply reflected Hispanics' own sense that they did not need exclusively ethnic-based mediating structures to serve their interests. For example, working-class Mexican Americans may simply have preferred that unions represent them (Mexican Americans had indeed been active in unions and served in leadership positions for many years, particularly in the Steelworkers, United Auto Workers, Meatpackers, and other industrial unions in the Midwest and the Southwest, as well as the United Farm Workers Union in California). In some cases, certainly, Hispanics used the church to mediate their grievances. And aspiring middle-class Hispanics either joined local business and civic groups or their own organizations, such as LULAC. That most of these Hispanic civic groups pursued assimilationist goals may not have satisfied the expectations of the Ford Foundation, but it seemed to suit their members' desires and interests. Nonetheless, the foundation, with the advice of a handful of Mexican American activists, decided that it would step in to create new institutions to serve the Hispanic community.

Over the years, the Ford Foundation has continued to provide the major funding for several Hispanic groups and has virtually created several organizations. It has given more than $9.6 million to the National Council of La Raza and $14.2 million to MALDEF since 1968.[21] A roster of Ford-supported Hispanic groups reads like a Who's Who of Hispanic political organizations. In 1968 the foundation gave money to ASPIRA, a Puerto Rican education group in New York, to allow it to replicate its activities outside New York; in 1972 the foundation helped create the Puerto Rican Legal Defense and Education Fund; in 1974, it provided operating funds for the Southwest Voter Registration Education Project and later the Midwest Voter Registration Education Project. Other Hispanic organizations and programs that have received large Ford Foundation grants include the Hispanic Policy Development Project, the NALEO Education Fund, the National Puerto Rican Coalition, and the Hispanic Leadership Opportunity Program, which provides internships in government agencies and policy research organizations. In addition, the foundation has contributed to a variety of academic programs for Hispanics, including grants to the City University of New York, for the Inter-University Program on Latino Research; the University of Texas and the University of Michigan, for a national survey of Hispanic political views, attitudes, and behavior. In 1970 it established a graduate fellowship program for Mexican American and Puerto Rican students and a minority postdoctoral fellowship program at the National Academy of Sciences. Outside the public policy arena, it also gave substantial support to organizations in the Hispanic community to promote economic development, including the Spanish Speaking Unity Council in Oakland, California, the Mexican American Unity Council in San Antonio, Texas, and Chicanos Por La Causa in Phoenix, Arizona.[22]

Other foundations joined Ford in funding Hispanic organizations and causes, including Carnegie and Rockefeller, as well as other, less well-known foundations and the philanthropic arms of corporations such as Kellogg, Anheuser-Busch, and Coors. For a time during the 1970s, the federal government also provided funding to some Hispanic organizations through grants for job training and other programs from the U.S. Department of Labor and other federal agencies. Both the Nixon and the Carter administrations used grants to Hispanic groups in an attempt to increase their political leverage within the Hispanic community. But neither the federal government nor any foundation matched the Ford Foundation in terms of long-term commitment or total amount of money contributed. Indeed, the Ford Foundation virtually created the infrastructure of the contemporary Hispanic policy movement.

According to Henry Santiestevan, a former United Auto Workers official who later headed the Ford-funded Southwest Council of La Raza, "without the Ford Foundation's commitment to a strategy of national and local institution-building, the Chicano Movement would have withered away in many areas, unable to overcome its desperate lack of resources and the often savage attacks of hostile external interests."[23] Siobhan Oppenheimer Nicolau, a former Ford Foundation program officer who guided Ford's early decisions to fund Hispanic organizations, has explained why Mexican Americans were unable to create and sustain their own network of viable institutions:

They lacked the strong network of religious institutions that had nurtured Black leadership. They lacked visibility outside the Southwest, and they lacked a history of slavery, a powerful tool that had galvanized White guilt and support for the Black civil rights movement.[24]

Nicolau is correct about one thing: blacks and Hispanics have had very different histories in the United States. This is one reason why organizations comparable to the major black civil rights groups have never developed in the Hispanic community.

Hispanics have not faced the same degree or intensity of discrimination in this society as blacks, despite the claims of many Hispanic activists and leaders. That is not to say that Hispanics have been free from discrimination at the hands of non-Hispanics, only that the comparison with discrimination against blacks overstates the case. Segregationist Jim Crow laws did not cover Mexican Americans, for example. Although Hispanic children were routinely segregated from non-Hispanics in south Texas and even sporadically in California, such segregation was not sanctioned by law and was struck down when challenged. As early as 1931, Mexican American parents in San Diego, California, won the right to send their children to school with non-Hispanics where local officials had attempted to deny it.[25] In one of the most rigorous measures of social acceptance—intermarriage rates—Mexican Americans are far more likely to marry non-Hispanics than blacks are to marry whites, and their intermarriage rates have increased over time. Only about 20 percent of the Mexican Americans in Los Angeles County married outside the group in 1924; in the early 1960s more than 40 percent did. Statewide in California, intermarriage rates are even higher, with more than half of all Mexican Americans marrying non-Hispanics.[26]

The role of foundations in the creation and maintenance of the major Hispanic organizations is of more than academic interest. Over the last twenty years, these organizations, especially MALDEF, have played an enormous role in shaping public policy toward Hispanics, in everything from education to immigration policy and voting laws. During the first seven years of its operation, from 1968 to 1975, MALDEF emerged as a major player on the public policy scene, especially in education. In addition to fighting for bilingual education for Mexican American students (*Serna* v. *Portales*, 1972), the organization took on desegregation cases and First Amendment suits. In Colorado, Texas, and California, MALDEF defended Mexican American student protesters who had been expelled for organizing school walkouts (or "blowouts," as they were known in the vernacular of the time). MALDEF also became a leading advocate of school finance reform, filing suits in state and federal court that claimed that school finance schemes based on the property tax were unconstitutional. The argument was rejected by the U.S. Supreme Court in *San Antonio Independent School District* v. *Rodriguez* (1973), but MALDEF was far more successful in state courts. In a suit filed in California, *Serrano* v. *Priest* (1971), the state supreme court ruled that California's constitution did not permit the quality of a child's education to be determined by the wealth of his parents and neighbors. MALDEF's influence in this arena was extensive, for some twenty-eight states ultimately passed school finance reform laws.[27]

MALDEF used the courts as a powerful vehicle to promote public policy, as did other Hispanic organizations funded by the Ford Foundation. ASPIRA, a Puerto Rican Ford Foundation grantee, was instrumental in promoting bilingual education in the public schools of New York City after it filed suit against the school system, which was settled by a consent decree that guaranteed all Hispanic students in the school system the right to bilingual education. The Puerto Rican Legal Defense Fund, which filed the ASPIRA case, has also been an active litigant in voting rights and bilingual education cases in New York, Illinois, and elsewhere. These organizations, like other public interest groups in the last three decades, found that in an era of growing judicial activism, sweeping changes could be brought about by litigating an issue. Even when legislation was ultimately called for, as in the area of school finance reform, the initial groundwork was often laid in the courts.

These organizations, for all their influence on public policy toward Hispanics, are not directly accountable to the community whose interests they purport to represent. The Hispanic community does not elect the leaders of these organizations, most of whom remain unknown in the larger Hispanic community. Few Mexican Americans could name the leader of even one of the major Mexican American policy groups—or perhaps give the names of the groups themselves.[28] The Hispanic community does not control the funding of the groups and, most important, has virtually no say in the agenda they choose to promote. By freeing these organizations from the need to be accountable to the communities they are supposed to represent, the Ford Foundation has created a cadre of ethnic power brokers rather than legitimate representatives of the Hispanic community.

These groups consider themselves to be on the cutting edge of social change, but the future they envision for Hispanics is one in which Hispanics attain permanent entitlement status based on ethnicity. It is not one in which Hispanics, like other groups before them, choose to become part of the mainstream. These groups frequently speak of "empowering" Hispanics, but it is difficult to imagine how defining Hispanics as members of a "protected class" will achieve that aim. Winning court battles to have Hispanic children taught in Spanish in a society in which the best jobs go to people who speak, read, and write English well hardly empowers Hispanic youngsters. Insisting that the political fortunes of middle-class Hispanics must be determined by the most disadvantaged Hispanics does not empower either group, but makes the former hostage to the misfortunes of the latter. The only groups that benefit from such misguided policy objectives are those that broker the policies in the first place.

CHAPTER 4

The Backlash

Hispanic organizations have been tremendously successful in having their political agenda endorsed by courts and legislative bodies in the last twenty years, but the public has proven more skeptical. When Miami's mayor Maurice Ferré boasted in a newspaper interview, "Within ten years there will not be a word of English spoken [in Miami] ... one day residents will have to learn Spanish or leave," his comments sent shock waves even through liberal circles.[1] As Hispanic organizations demanded that American institutions change to accommodate Hispanics rather than the other way around, they provided fodder to those who would prefer that Hispanics not be accepted as fully participating members of the society in the first place. Predictably, the most strident demands of Hispanics for special treatment have provoked a backlash, which has been getting stronger in recent years.

The backlash can be ugly. After writing a newspaper opinion piece on the progress of Hispanics in the United States, I received a number of anonymous letters. A typical one suggested,

Isn't it incredible, outrageous, preposterous that we have to fight to retain our "native" language? That foreigners seek to take over, overrun OUR country? What the hell was the Alamo fought for? Texas is fast becoming BIG ... Mexico and Florida has long since become BIG ... CUBA. Less than ten miles from me, Union City [New Jersey] boasts of having "The largest Cuban population outside of Miami." Two miles from me, Paterson, is a haven for all of South America and the entire Caribbean.... I really think the bricks for a wall across our ENTIRE southern border should be on their way south NOW. WHY wait until it is—TOO LATE?

Not all those who form this backlash are cranks and xenophobes. Many are simply frustrated at what they see as an erosion in the consensus that the United States has a common language and culture worth preserving. They see Hispanic youngsters taught in their native language, ballots printed in Spanish, and licensing exams for everything from becoming a barber to driving a car administered in Spanish. They see election districts gerrymandered to give Hispanics extra political clout, illegal aliens used to apportion legislative seats, and even demands by some Hispanic leaders that noncitizens be allowed to vote in U.S. elections. They see Hispanics given preference in hiring, promotions, and admission to universities. At some point, non-Hispanics were bound to ask why Hispanics deserve such special treatment. And the most outraged were bound to try to do something about it. The outrage has been manifest in laws to make English the official language and in attempts to restrict Hispanic immigration. Neither of these efforts, however, has addressed head-on the issue of Hispanic entitlements. Moreover, both have polarized the Hispanic community, driving many moderate Hispanics into a more radical, separatist camp.

A COMMON LANGUAGE, THE TIE THAT BINDS

Nothing so stirs animosity toward Hispanics as the belief that they do not wish to learn English. Although the United States has no official language, as about half of the countries in the world do, English has been the common language for our entire history as a nation.[2] While enclaves of non-English-speaking immigrants have existed throughout that history, most immigrants, especially those of the great migrations of this century, adopted English quickly, usually within one or two generations.[3] The demand for bilingual education, voting materials, even pilot-license exams in Spanish has irritated many Americans whose own grandparents managed to learn English and would not have dreamed of demanding that the citizens of their adopted country be forced to communicate with them in their native language. The proliferation of programs and services in Spanish, coupled with increasingly strident demands by Hispanic leaders that Hispanics remain separate and distinct within this society, brought a reaction in the guise of a simple, two-sentence proposed amendment to the U.S. Constitution.

S. I. Hayakawa, a one-term Republican senator from California, introduced a Senate joint resolution in 1981 to amend the Constitution to make English the official language of the United States. It declared,

Section 1. The English language shall be the official language of the United States.

Section 2. The Congress shall have the power to enforce this article by appropriate legislation.

Senator Hayakawa's amendment was cosponsored by ten other senators but, like most legislation introduced, died without being acted on in the Ninety-seventh Congress. Nonetheless, it gave impetus to a national, grass-roots organization, U.S. English, of which Hayakawa became honorary chairman when he retired from the Senate in 1983 (and of which I later became president).

In many respects, Hayakawa was an unlikely leader of such an organization. He was an immigrant, born in Canada to parents of Japanese origin; a former college professor and president; and a renowned semanticist. As such, he did not fit the nativist image often associated with those who tried to protect English.

The nativist approach was not new. In 1923, for example, the U.S. Supreme Court struck down a Nebraska law restricting teaching in a foreign language below the eighth grade. Anti-German sentiment in the post–World War I era was largely responsible for this ill-conceived law, which went far beyond modern legislative efforts to give special recognition to English.

Since 1983, when U.S. English was founded, fourteen states have passed laws declaring English their official language, in five cases through popular initiatives or referenda.[4] U.S. English now numbers some 400,000 members and has a total budget of about $6 million annually.[5] Moreover, U.S. English is not the only such organization; English First, a group with more conservative ties, claims 250,000 members and a budget of about $1.5 million, and other local and state groups promote efforts to declare English the official language.

The real fear of many Americans is that Hispanics will one day be a group large and powerful enough to insist that the United States adopt a bilingual language policy. That fear is not so far-fetched, as Canada's example demonstrates. French Canadians make up only about one-quarter of the Canadian population, but they have succeeded in forcing the entire country to recognize and use French as an official language— even while radical Francophones in Quebec outlaw the use of English on outdoor signs on private establishments. (Canada is experiencing its most serious secession crises in its history since some English-speaking provinces refused to ratify an agreement to grant special status to Quebec and to allow it greater provincial autonomy.) Will something similar happen with Spanish when nearly one-third of the U.S. population is Hispanic? The mere possibility drives some Americans to try to make sure that day does not come.

The first major victory in U.S. English's efforts to pass statewide initiatives occurred in 1986 in California. Proposition 63, which declared that "English is the Official Language of California," received 73 percent of the popular vote. In 1988 U.S. English and its state affiliates won approval of three additional popular initiatives in Arizona, Colorado, and Florida; in 1990 they sponsored an Alabama referendum, bringing to eighteen the number of states that have recognized English as their official language.[6] The political battle to pass such initiatives, however, has become increasingly bitter, inflaming public opinion in both the Hispanic and the non-Hispanic communities.

ARIZONA AND THE ANTI–OFFICIAL ENGLISH REBOUND

The 1988 campaigns, in particular, drew fire from public officials, and in Arizona the state initiative failed to generate as much popular support as initiatives in other states had. Although Arizona voters adopted English as the state's official language, the vote was close, 51 percent to 49 percent, compared with votes of 84 to 11 in Florida and of 61 to 39 in Colorado.[7] Arizonans against Official English, a coalition opposition group, not only marshaled an impressive array of spokesmen against the initiative—including both U.S. senators, the Democrat Dennis DeConcini and the Republican

John McCain—but was well financed and able to run television advertisements. One ad began with pictures showing
"Official English" signs and a voice warning, "It always starts
like this . . ." These slowly turned into pictures of Senator
Joseph McCarthy, Adolf Hitler, and concentration camp victims being led into the gas chamber.[8] The efforts of Arizonans
against Official English were effective. Support for the Arizona initiative eroded significantly during the campaign. Elsewhere, too, politicians ran for cover on the English-language
issue. Both presidential candidates, George Bush and Michael
Dukakis, publicly opposed "English only" laws, as did Jesse
Jackson.[9]

In all of the campaigns to make English the official language, opponents charged that such efforts were motivated
by racism and that Hispanics' right to speak Spanish in public would be curtailed by the laws. It is true that some advocates of the most extreme "English only" sentiment would
probably bar the use of Spanish in private enterprises as
well as in public institutions if they could. A citizens' group
in Monterey Park, California, attempted to prohibit non-
English signs (in this case, mostly in Korean and other Asian
languages) on private establishments that catered to an almost exclusively ethnic clientele, and some employers have
attempted to prevent employees from speaking Spanish during their breaks.[10] But most proponents of official-English
laws are not concerned with the private use of Spanish.
What they object to is the increasing use of Spanish by
government and its institutions, what amounts to acceptance
of Spanish as a second language in many parts of the country. Official-English proponents are objecting not to Hispanic parents' offering after-school or Saturday classes in
Spanish so that Hispanic children can maintain their native
language but the state's being required to do so at public
expense.

THE U.S. ENGLISH FLAP

In October 1988 I resigned as president of U.S. English, after serving in that position for about fourteen months. I had originally accepted the job because I believed bilingual education and similar policies have been a disaster for Hispanics and the country, despite my reservation that a constitutional amendment or laws to make English the official language would probably not do much to address this problem. I thought an organization was needed that could at least challenge the powerful lobby supporting such policies, and I was willing to lead it, even though I knew that many of my fellow Hispanics would criticize me. I was comforted by the fact that the board of advisers of the organization included such well-known persons as Walter Cronkite, Alistair Cooke, Saul Bellow, Norman Podhoretz, Jacques Barzun, and George Gilder, none of whom could be accused of being racist or xenophobic (Gilder, in fact, is an outspoken advocate of increasing immigration to the United States).

Unfortunately, others associated with U.S. English turned out to carry more political baggage. Its founder, John Tanton, an ophthalmologist from Michigan, also founded the Federation of American Immigration Reform, a much smaller organization—it claims 50,000 members—but one that has played a pivotal role in immigration policy. Tanton favors rigid restriction of immigration and is particularly anxious to limit the number of low-skilled Latin immigrants coming to the United States. In 1986, in what surely was a reckless moment, he committed his fears about Latin immigrants to paper in a memo intended to be circulated privately among some colleagues in the immigration restriction movement. Much of the memo raised legitimate issues, but some of it reflected a demonstrably anti-Hispanic bias. Tanton questioned the "educability" of Hispanics and wrote of a "Latin onslaught" that would threaten the ability of blacks "to im-prove (or even maintain) their position." He asked rhetori-cally, "Will Latin American migrants bring with them the tradition of the *mordida* (bribe), the lack of involvement in public affairs, etc?" Perhaps most offensively, however, he wrote,

Can *homo contraceptivus* compete with *homo progenitiva* if borders aren't controlled? Or is advice to limit ones [*sic*] family simply advice to move over and let someone else with greater reproductive powers occupy the space? . . . On the demographic point: perhaps this is the first instance in which those with their pants up are going to get caught by those with their pants down![11]

The memo had been written a year before I joined the organization, and neither I nor members of the advisory board were aware of its existence until an article in the *Arizona Republic* in October 1988 made its contents available. Walter Cronkite resigned, and so did I, within days of learn-ing of the memo, which struck me as anti-Hispanic. That the chairman of U.S. English had written it compromised, I felt, my ability to refute charges that the organization itself was xenophobic. Tanton resigned immediately after I did.

To many Hispanic organizations, the Tanton memo was clear proof that concerns about bilingualism were really be-ing driven by racism. As a *Time* magazine article noted, "Op-ponents of the official-English movement consider it to be no more than a socially acceptable way of tapping into xenopho-bic fears: fears of being outnumbered by immigrants, fear that jobs are in jeopardy from cheap labor, just plain fear of anyone different."[12] What Hispanic leaders would not enter-tain was the possibility that their own actions and rhetoric were spreading such fear faster than anything U.S. English could possibly do. In 1974 a Hispanic official in the Carter administration testified before a congressional subcommittee that in the near future the United States should consider providing all government services in both English and Spanish, as in the Canadian model.[13] In 1978, according to *Time*, Emmy Shafer became the first public "English-only" advocate when "she could not find a clerk in the Dade County [Florida] municipal offices who could speak English to her."[14] In 1985 an Arizona state legislator proposed a state resolution that would prohibit "persons who do not speak a native language indigenous to the region, or who are not descendants of persons living in the area prior to the [Gadsden] purchase, from residing in the territory acquired under the Gadsden Purchase Act of 1853."[15] Year in and year out, Americans were being told by Hispanic leaders that Hispanics could not, or would not, follow in the footsteps of previous immigrants. The "official-English movement" marked one attempt to force the issue; by winning passage of state amendments, it would put the American people on record as favoring the retention of a common language.

Ironically, despite the ominous warnings of opponents and the claims of proponents, official-English laws have had virtually no impact on public policy. States that provide Spanish ballots in state elections (which is not required by federal law) have continued to do so even where, as in California, state law now mandates English as the official language of government. State bilingual education policy mandating native-language instructions for Hispanic children has remained intact despite official-English laws, as have all other native-language services in each of the states. Efforts to alter official bilingual policy through legislation making English the official language have proved largely unsuccessful. Other individuals, like Tanton, have proposed different tactics to deal with the problem.

CLOSING THE BORDERS

The former Colorado governor Richard Lamm, an activist in the movement to restrict immigration, warns, "I know that earlier large waves of immigrants didn't 'overturn' America, but there are ... reasons to believe that today's migration is different from earlier flows."[16] Others make ominous references to the Latinization of America. The novelist Edward Abbey, in his essay "Immigration and Liberal Taboos," asks, "How many of us, truthfully, would prefer to be submerged in the Caribbean-Latin version of civilization?"[17] Thomas Fleming, editor of the journal *Chronicles*, warns, "A United States dominated by Third World immigrants will be a very different nation in its cultural and its economic life." He adds, "More fruit pickers we do not need," in an obvious—though erroneous—reference to Mexican immigrants.[18]

These sentiments reflect the mood of a growing immigration restriction movement. In 1986, opponents of immigration succeeded in passing a law to try to restrict illegal immigration by penalizing employers who hire illegal aliens. (The Immigration Reform and Control Act of 1986 is dealt with more fully in chapter 6, along with other issues related to immigrants.) However, immigration restrictionists have had more difficulty passing laws to limit legal immigration, in part because legislators and the public have a strong attachment to the notion that the United States is, and should continue to be, a nation of immigrants. But most Americans support immigration with a caveat—the expectation that immigrants adapt themselves to the language, values, and mores of this nation. It is a social contract between the person welcomed into the home and the host: when in Rome, do as the Romans do. When Hispanics insist that they do not have to follow the same rules as every group before them, they threaten this contract.

HISPANICS AND LANGUAGE RIGHTS

Neither the popularity and success of the official-English movement nor the threat of the growing movement to restrict immigration has stimulated any rethinking of tactics or rhetoric on the part of Hispanic activists. If anything, the campaigns for official-English laws have polarized many of the communities that have taken them up, with moderate Hispanics joining the ranks of some of the more radical exponents of Hispanic separatism in arguing that Hispanics are entitled to have their language and culture maintained at public expense. Hispanic groups now routinely call for recognition of minority "language rights" that go far beyond simple First Amendment protection (which has usually been interpreted to apply to the content of speech, not the form of expression chosen). The establishment of language rights for minorities would effectively make multi-lingualism the language policy of the United States. It would not only obligate the government to provide universal services in the native languages of language minorities but also protect the right of those minorities to use their native languages in all situations. For example, the First Amendment is not usually interpreted as granting protection to employees to speak whatever language they choose on the job.[19] But laws establishing language rights would confer far broader *employee* discretion under such circumstances.

Some proponents of language rights go so far as to seek to amend civil rights statutes to prohibit "the fail[ure] or refus[al] to hire or to discharge, or otherwise to discriminate against any individual ... because of such individual's race, color, religion, sex, *language* [emphasis added] or national origin."[20] But language is quite different from such characteristics as race or gender, which are immutable. With the exception of religion, which historically has separate claims to protection, only immutable characteristics were granted special protection under traditional civil rights laws. Employers are forbidden from discriminating on the basis of such characteristics as race and gender, in part because for them to do so would be inherently unfair, since persons cannot change their gender or race. But language is learned, and employers have traditionally been given broad discretion to "discriminate" between employees on the basis of learned knowledge. A car repair shop is free to employ only people who know how to repair engines, for example; an office manager may hire only secretaries who know how to type; a hospital may decide to hire only doctors who know how to perform brain surgery for its neurological surgery department; and so on. The demand that employers be forbidden from considering whether a potential employee speaks English is a far more radical claim than any previously made in the name of civil rights.

WHAT THE FUTURE HOLDS

Despite increased economic mobility and social integration, the Hispanic population will very likely remain a distinct subgroup, or subgroups, for years to come, especially as increasing numbers of Hispanic immigrants are added to the pool. Ethnic identification is tenacious. A recent survey of predominantly foreign-born Hispanics found that more than 80 percent describe themselves as "Hispanic first/American second," and the number of Hispanics claiming primary allegiance to their ethnic group has been increasing over the past several years.[21] But Hispanics will not simply transfer the culture of Mexico, Puerto Rico, Cuba, El Salvador, the Dominican Republic, and more than a dozen other countries to the United States. Their ethnic identity will be shaped by their experiences in the United States. As Nathan Glazer and Daniel Patrick Moynihan have explained, "ethnic groups, owing to their distinctive historical experiences, their cultures and skills, the times of their arrival and the economic situation they met, developed distinctive economic, political, and cultural patterns. As the old culture fell away—and it did rapidly enough—a new one, shaped by the distinctive experiences of life in America, was formed and a new identity created."[22] Indeed, the creation of a *Hispanic* identity (as opposed to a Mexican, a Puerto Rican, or a Cuban identity) is an example of the phenomenon Glazer and Moynihan described.

Certainly our public policies will play a role in determining what identity Hispanics choose. Those policies have been decidedly less assimilationist in recent years than in the past. Although the pressure to adopt the cultural norms and values of the dominant society will always be powerful, as the "dominant" (non-Hispanic white) group diminishes in places like Los Angeles and Miami, so will the pressure to adapt to values and norms held by a shrinking percentage of the population. Some alarmists predict disaster. One recently declared, "It is quite clear that it is no longer realistic to assume that this vast and growing number of immigrants, who also prove to be more prolific in child-bearing than the native white American population, are likely to comply with the cultural ideal of conformity to 'Old American' ideals and institutions."[23] Such statements exaggerate the threat, but it would be foolish to ignore the social impact of twenty years of accommodation to a more pluralist model of American culture.

According to one survey, Hispanics themselves believe that they are demanding and getting more "respect for and recognition of their culture."[24] But if recognition and respect are merely indifference to Hispanics' remaining outside the mainstream, Hispanics will be the losers. In the past, ethnic groups fought to be accepted into the American mainstream, often against the wishes of nativists, who would have been content to allow ethnics to remain "outsiders." But the process of becoming accepted always entailed trade-offs for members of ethnic groups. It meant, for one thing, switching allegiance from one's country of birth or ancestry to the United States. (After all, the oath taken during naturalization requires the alien to "renounce and abjure all allegiance and fidelity to any foreign prince, potentate, state or sovereignty" of which he or she was a subject or citizen.[25]) But ethnic minorities were willing to pay the price because the benefits of assimilation ultimately included a greater degree of economic mobility and social integration.

Hispanics demand economic parity. They seek the right to live where they choose; they want equal access to education and other social benefits for themselves and their children. They want the right to participate in the political process. In other words, they seek full and open admission into the American community—to which they are certainly entitled. On the other side of the ledger, the community has traditionally expected all persons seeking to join it to make certain accommodations, not least of which is the adoption of the common language. That does not mean that all Hispanics must give up Spanish. It does mean that Hispanics living in the United States should eventually embrace English as *their* language, too, just as German Americans, Italian Americans, Jews, and others did before them.

If Hispanics choose, as many Greek Americans and other select ethnics have, to maintain their native language for use within their families, communities, and churches, they must accept full responsibility for doing so. Hispanics cannot insist, as many of their leaders do, that the larger community must bend to their demand for public recognition of Spanish and that it must pay to preserve Spanish among one segment of the population. Nor should Hispanics expect Americans willingly to abandon more than two hundred years of tradition as a unilingual society. A bilingual future is simply not in the cards. To continue to push for broader public acceptance of Spanish will simply provoke an even bigger backlash than has already occurred.

CHAPTER 5

An Emerging Middle Class

"Each decade offered us hope, but our hopes evaporated into smoke. We became the poorest of the poor, the most segregated minority in schools, the lowest paid group in America and the least educated minority in this nation."[1] This view of Hispanics' progress by the president of the National Council of La Raza, one of the country's leading Hispanic civil rights groups, is the prevalent one among Hispanic leaders and is shared by many outside the Hispanic community as well. By and large, Hispanics are perceived to be a disadvantaged minority—poorly educated, concentrated in barrios, economically impoverished; with little hope of participating in the American Dream. This perception has not changed substantially in twenty-five years. And it is wrong.

Hispanics have been called the invisible minority, and indeed they were for many years, largely because most Hispanics lived in the Southwest and the Northeast, away from the most blatant discrimination of the Deep South. But the most invisible Hispanics today are those who have been absorbed into the mainstream. The success of middle-class Hispanics is an untold—and misunderstood—story perhaps least appreciated by Hispanic advocates whose interest is in promoting the view that Latinos cannot make it in this society.

The Hispanic poor, who constitute only about one-fourth of the Hispanic population, are visible to all. These are the Hispanics most likely to be studied, analyzed, and reported on and certainly the ones most likely to be read about. A recent computer search of stories about Hispanics in major newspapers and magazines over a twelve-month period turned up more than eighteen hundred stories in which the word *Hispanic* or *Latino* occurred within a hundred words of the word *poverty*. In most people's minds, the expression *poor Hispanic* is almost redundant.

HAS HISPANICS' PROGRESS STALLED?

Most Hispanics, rather than being poor, lead solidly lower-middle- or middle-class lives, but finding evidence to support this thesis is sometimes difficult. Of course, Hispanic groups vary one from another, as do individuals within any group. Most analysts acknowledge, for example, that Cubans are highly successful. Within one generation, they have virtually closed the earnings and education gap with other Americans. (For a broad range of social and economic indicators for each of the major Hispanic groups, see table 1.) Although some analysts claim that the success of Cubans is due exclusively to their higher socioeconomic status when they arrived, many Cuban refugees—especially those who came after the first wave in the 1960s—were in fact skilled or semiskilled workers with relatively little education.[2] Their accomplishments in the United States are attributable in large measure to diligence and hard work. They established enclave economies, in the traditional immigrant mode, opening restaurants, stores, and other émigré-oriented services. Some Cubans were able to get a foothold in industries not usually available to immigrants. They formed banks, specializing in international transactions attuned to Latin American as well as local customers, and

Table 1: Characteristics of Hispanic Subgroups and Non-Hispanics

	Mexican-origin*	Puerto Rican	Cuban	South/Central American	Other Hispanic	Non-Hispanic
Total population (in millions)	13.3	2.2	1.0	2.8	1.4	246.2
Median age	24.1	27.0	39.1	28.0	31.1	33.5
Median years of schooling (1988)	10.8	12	12.4	12.4	12.7	12.7
Percentage in labor force						
Male	81.2%	69.2%	74.9%	83.7%	75.3%	74.2%
Female	52.9%	41.4%	57.8%	61.0%	57.0%	57.4%
Percentage of unemployed	9.0%	8.6%	5.8%	6.6%	6.2%	5.3%
Median earnings (1989)						
Male	$12,527	$18,222	$19,336	$15,067	$17,486	$22,081
Female	$8,874	$12,812	$12,880	$10,083	$11,564	$11,885
Percentage of married-couple families	72.5%	57.2%	77.4%	68.7%	69.8%	79.9%
Percentage of female-headed families	19.6%	38.9%	18.9%	25.0%	24.5%	16.0%
Percentage of out-of-wedlock births	28.9%	53.0%	16.1%	37.1%	34.2%	23.9%**
Percentage of families in poverty	25.7%	30.4%	12.5%	16.8%	15.8%	9.2%

SOURCES: Bureau of the Census, *The Hispanic Population in the United States: March 1990*, Current Population Reports, ser. P-20, no. 449; median years of schooling are from *The Hispanic Population of the United States: March 1988*, Current Population Reports, ser. P-20, no. 438; out-of-wedlock births are from National Center for Health Statistics, *Advance Report of Final Natality Statistics, 1987*.

*Mexican-origin population includes both native- and foreign-born persons.

**Includes black out-of-wedlock births, 63.1% and white births, 13.9%.

made major investments in real estate development in south Florida. These ventures provided big profits for only a few Cubans but jobs for many more. By 1980 Miami boasted some two hundred Cuban millionaires and 18,000 Cuban-owned businesses, and about 70 percent of all Cubans there owned their own homes (a rate that exceeds that of whites generally).[3] But Cubans are as a rule dismissed as the exception among Hispanics. What about other Hispanic groups? Why has there been no "progress" among them?

The largest and most important group is the Mexican American population. As earlier chapters showed, its leaders have driven much of the policy agenda affecting all Hispanics, but the importance of Mexican Americans also stems from their having a longer history in the United States than does any other Hispanic group. If Mexican Americans whose families have lived in the United States for generations are not yet making it in this society, they may have a legitimate claim to consider themselves a more or less permanently disadvantaged group, like blacks. That is precisely what Mexican American leaders suggest is happening. Their proof is that statistical measures of Mexican American achievement in education, earnings, poverty rates, and other social and economic indicators have remained largely unchanged for decades. In 1959 the median income of Mexican-origin males in the Southwest was 57 percent that of non-Hispanics.[4] In 1989 it was still 57 percent of non-Hispanic income.[5] If Mexican Americans had made progress, it would show up in improved education attainment and earnings and in lower poverty rates, so the argument goes. Since it doesn't, progress must be stalled.

In the post–civil rights era, the failure of a minority to close the social and economic gap with whites is assumed to be the result of persistent discrimination. Progress is perceived not in absolute but in relative terms. The poor may become less poor over time, but so long as those on the upper rungs of the economic ladder are climbing even faster, the poor are believed to have suffered some harm, even if they have made absolute gains and their lives are much improved. However, in order for Hispanics (or any group on the lower rungs) to close the gap, they must progress at an even greater rate than non-Hispanic whites; their apparent failure to do so in recent years causes Hispanic leaders and the public to conclude that Hispanics are falling behind. Is this a fair way to judge Hispanics' progress? In fact, it makes almost no sense to apply this test today (if it ever did), because the Hispanic population itself is changing so rapidly. This is most true of the Mexican-origin population.

In 1959 the overwhelming majority of persons of Mexican origin living in the United States were native-born, 85 percent. Today only about two-thirds of the people of Mexican origin were born in the United States, and among adults barely one in two was born here. Increasingly, the Hispanic population, including that of Mexican origin, is made up of new immigrants, who, like immigrants of every era, start off at the bottom of the economic ladder. This infusion of new immigrants is bound to distort our image of progress in the Hispanic population, if each time we measure the group we include people who have just arrived and have yet to make their way in this society.

A simple analogy illustrates the point. Suppose we compared the achievement of two classes of students in the same grade as measured by a standardized test administered at the beginning and the end of the school year, but the only information by which we could assess progress was the mean score for the class. Let's say that the mean score for Class A was 100 points on the initial test, a score right at the national average, and that Class B scored 75. In the test given at the end of the school year, Class A scored 150 (again the national average) and Class B scored 110. Both classes made progress, but Class B still had not eliminated the gap between it and Class A and remained significantly below the national average. Having only this information, we would be justified in believing that students in Class B were continuing to lag in educational achievement.

But suppose we discovered that Class B had grown by one-half by the time the second test was given and that the other class had remained stable. In Class A thirty students took the test at the beginning of the school year, and the same thirty took it at the end. In Class B, however, fifteen new students were added to the class between the first and the second test. We would have no way of knowing what the average final test score meant in terms of the overall achievement of students in Class B until we knew more about the new students. Suppose we then found out that half of them were recent, non-English-speaking immigrants. We could reasonably assume that the addition of even five such students would skew the test results for the entire class, presumably lowering the class mean. Unless we had more information, though, we still wouldn't know what exact effect the scores of the new students had on the class mean or how much progress the original students had actually made over the year.

Hispanics in the United States—and the Mexican-origin population in particular—are very much like Class B. In 1980 there were about 14.6 million Hispanics living in the United States; in 1990, nearly 21 million, an increase of about 44 percent in one decade. At least one-half of this increase was the result of immigration, legal and illegal. As chapter 6 details, this influx consists mostly of poorly educated persons, with minimal skills, who cannot speak English. Not surprisingly, when these Hispanics are added to the pool being measured, the achievement levels of the whole group fall. It is almost inconceivable that the addition of two or three million new immigrants to the Hispanic pool would not seriously distort evidence of Hispanics' progress during the decade. Yet no major Hispanic organization will acknowledge the validity of this reasonable assumption. Instead, Hispanic leaders complain, "Hispanics are the population that has benefitted least from the economic recovery."[6] "The Myth of Hispanic Progress" is the title of a study by a Mexican American professor, purporting to show that "it is simply wrong to assume that Hispanics are making gradual progress towards parity with Anglos."[7] "Hispanic poverty is now comparable to that of blacks and is expected to exceed it by the end of this decade," warns another group.[8]

Hispanics wear disadvantage almost like a badge of distinction, as if groups were competing with each other for the title "most disadvantaged." Sadly, the most frequently heard complaint among Hispanic leaders is not that the public ignores evidence of Hispanics' achievement but that it underestimates their disadvantage. "More than any group in American political history, Hispanic Americans have turned to the national statistical system as an instrument for advancing their political and economic interests, by making visible the magnitude of social and economic problems they face," says a Rockefeller Foundation official.[9] But gathering all Hispanics together under one umbrella obscures as much information as it illuminates, and may make Hispanics—especially the native-born—appear to suffer greater social and economic problems than they actually do.

In fact, a careful examination of the voluminous data on the Hispanic population gathered by the Census Bureau and other federal agencies shows that, as a group, Hispanics have made progress in this society and that most of them have moved into the social and economic mainstream. In most respects, Hispanics—particularly those born here—are very much like other Americans: they work hard, support their own families without outside assistance, have more education and higher earnings than their parents, and own their own home. In short, they are pursuing the American Dream—with increasing success.

THE FAMILY

No institution is more important to the success of Hispanics (or any group) than the family. The breakdown of the black family over the last several decades signaled the most serious threat to the progress of blacks since Jim Crow. But Hispanics—with the exception of Puerto Ricans, who are discussed in chapter 7—do not appear to be in danger of experiencing a similar decline in the vitality of the traditional family. About 73 percent of all Mexican-origin families and 77 percent of all Cuban families consist of married couples, a rate comparable to that of all whites (80 percent). Only 20 percent of the Mexican-origin and 19 percent of the Cuban families are headed by women with no husband present. While out-of-wedlock births to Mexican-origin women are higher than those to white women generally, 29 percent compared with 14 percent, they fall considerably short of the 63 percent of such births to black women; and the Hispanic children born out of wedlock are still likely to grow up in families with two parents. The babies of Mexican-origin women, even those who have received little or no prenatal care, are generally quite healthy; the babies of foreign-born Mexican mothers have a lower infant mortality rate and lower incidence of low birth weight, a common predictor of health problems, than those of blacks or whites. While researchers are not sure what accounts for the apparent health of even poor Mexican babies, one reason may be that their mothers are less likely to drink, smoke, or use drugs than white or black mothers and that Hispanic families place special emphasis on good nutrition for pregnant women.[10]

In general, Hispanic families are somewhat more traditional than non-Hispanic families; men are expected to work to support their families and women to care for children. Hispanic families tend to be child-centered, which increases the importance of women's role as child bearers.[11] Hispanic women are more likely to bear children early and to bear more children than their non-Hispanic peers.[12] Hispanics have a fertility rate higher than that of virtually any other group—non-Hispanic whites, blacks, or Asians.[13] Hispanic women are more likely to stay at home with their children than are women from other ethnic groups and are somewhat less likely to be in the labor force than white women generally.[14] With fewer Hispanic women working, Hispanic families are at a comparative disadvantage on measures of family income, because a higher percentage of non-Hispanic families consist of dual husband-wife earners. But the presence of Hispanic mothers in the home may provide other benefits to their families, including giving young children a nurturing and stable environment.

In another important way, Hispanic families tend to differ from many of their contemporary non-Hispanic counterparts. Hispanics are more likely than other Americans to believe that the demands and needs of the family should take precedence over those of the individual. In an earlier age this attitude was common among other ethnic groups—Italians, for example. Today, however, it runs counter to the dominant culture of individualism characteristic of American life and may even impede individual success. This perhaps explains why so many young Hispanics drop out of school to take jobs, a decision that has some immediate financial benefits for the family but is detrimental to the individual in the long run. Nonetheless, Hispanics' attachment to family is one of their most positive cultural attributes. Family members are expected to help each other in times of financial or other need, which some analysts believe explains why so many Mexican-origin families shun welfare even when their poverty makes them eligible for assistance.[15] The challenge for Hispanics will be maintaining a strong commitment to family while adapting to the demands of a society that rewards individual effort and achievement.

WORK

Hispanic men are more likely to be members of the labor force—that is, working or looking for work—than non-Hispanic whites. Among all Mexican-origin men sixteen years old or older in 1990, for example, participation in the labor force was substantially higher than it was for non-Hispanic males overall—81 percent compared with 74 percent.[16] This fact bodes well for the future and is in marked contrast to the experience of black men, whose labor force participation has been steadily declining for more than twenty years. Most analysts believe that low attachment to the labor force and its correlate, high dependence on welfare, are prime components of underclass behavior. As the political scientist Lawrence Mead writes in his book *Beyond Entitlement: The Social Obligations of Citizenship*, for many persons who are in the underclass, "the problem is not that jobs are *unavailable* but that they are frequently *unacceptable*, in pay or condition, given that some income is usually available from families or benefit programs."[17] In other words, persons in the underclass frequently choose not to work rather than to take jobs they deem beneath them. Of course, this attitude can prove as pernicious to the individual as poverty itself and virtually ensures that he will remain poor for longer than he would if he re-entered the labor force.[18] The willingness of Hispanic men to work, even at low-wage jobs if their skills qualify them for nothing better, suggests that Hispanics are in no immediate danger of forming a large underclass.

Hispanics' strong attachment to work is today important not only to their own achievement, but to society as well and will become even more so in the coming decades. Hispanics are a vital component of the American labor force. The 1980s were a period of tremendous job growth in the United States; nearly 19 million new jobs were created between 1980 and 1990, but non-Hispanic white men were becoming a smaller proportion of the work force at the same time. Had it not been for the influx of large numbers of women and Hispanic workers into the labor force in the last decade, the nation could not have sustained this great job expansion. During the 1980s, 3.3 million new Hispanic workers were added to the work force, giving Hispanics a disproportionate share of the new jobs. Hispanics benefited more than any other group in terms of employment growth in the last decade.[19] By the year 2000, they are expected to account for 10 percent of the nation's work force.

EARNINGS

Understandably, Hispanics and their leaders are concerned less with the impact of Hispanics on the labor force than with what has happened to their wages in this period. Hispanic leaders charge that Hispanics' wages have failed to keep pace with those of non-Hispanics. Statistics on average Hispanic earnings during the decade appear to bear this out, but they should be viewed with caution. The changing composition of the Hispanic population, from a predominantly native-born to an increasingly immigrant one, makes an enormous difference in how we interpret the data on Hispanic earnings. Since nearly half of all Hispanic workers are foreign-born and since many of these have immigrated within the last ten years, we should not be surprised that the average earnings of Hispanics appear low. After all, most Hispanic immigrants are semi-skilled workers who do not speak English, and their wages reflect these deficiencies. When huge numbers of such workers are added to the pool on which we base average-earnings figures, they will lower the mean, just as the new immigrant children lowered the mean test scores in the hypothetical case of Class B discussed above. Without being able to separate Hispanics who are native-born from those who are more recent immigrants, we cannot know precisely what effect the latter have on the average earnings for the whole group.

Unfortunately, mos: of the data published by the federal government do not distinguish between the earnings of native-born workers and those of immigrants, which leads many analysts to ignore the phenomenon altogether. There are, however, some unpublished government data that do provide such information, and my own analysis of them suggests that the average earnings of native-born Hispanics are commensurate with their education and skills and do not lag significantly behind those of comparable non-Hispanic whites.

In 1989 Hispanic men earned, on the average, about two-thirds as much a year as non-Hispanics, but there are wide differences in the average earnings of the various Hispanic groups, with Cuban males earning the most and Mexican-origin men the least. As we noted earlier, the data on the Mexican-origin population cause the most alarm among public policy analysts, since Mexicans are the largest and oldest group of Hispanics in the nation. Of course, this is also the group that has experienced the largest influx of immigrants into its ranks in the last decade. When earnings of native-born Mexican American men are analyzed separately from those of Mexican immigrants, a very different picture emerges. On the average, the weekly earnings of Mexican American men are about 83 percent those of non-Hispanic white men—a figure that cuts in half the apparent gap between their earnings and those of non-Hispanics.[20] Even this gap can be explained at least in part. Schooling, experience, hours worked, and geographical region of residence are among several factors that can affect earnings. When we compensate for these variables, we find that Mexican American men earn about 93 percent of the weekly earnings of comparable non-Hispanic white men.[21] English-language proficiency also plays an important role in the earnings of Hispanics; some economists assert that those who are proficient in English experience "no important earnings differences from native-born Anglos."[22]

Earnings alone do not convey the whole picture of Hispanics' progress, however. Educational attainment is probably the best indicator of future achievement, but here, too, conventional analysis fails to distinguish between Hispanics born and educated in the United States and those who immigrated here.

EDUCATION

Contrary to popular opinion, most Mexican American young adults have completed high school, being nearly as likely to do so as other Americans. But the popular press, the federal government, and Hispanic organizations cite statistics that indicate otherwise. They claim that about 60 percent of all Mexican-origin persons do not complete high school. The confusion stems, as it does with earnings data, from lumping native-born Hispanics with immigrants to get statistical averages for the entire group. Hispanic immigrants, especially Mexicans, are at an enormous disadvantage when it comes to education. Only half of all Mexican immigrants have completed seven or more years of schooling, and only 28 percent have completed twelve or more years (see table 2). Most of these immigrants came to the United States as young adults, after they had completed their formal education in Mexico. Including such persons in calculations of high school dropout rates for Hispanics greatly inflates these figures.

In fact, 78 percent of all second-generation Mexican American males aged twenty-five to thirty-four and 71 percent of the third-generation males have completed twelve or more years of education, compared with 90 percent of non-Hispanic whites in this age group. Among Mexican American men of all ages, a smaller percentage has completed high school, only 63 percent of all those over twenty-five. But even these figures

Table 2: Educational Attainment of 25- to 34-Year-Old
Mexican-Origin Males

Years of schooling completed	First generation	Second generation	Third generation	Non-Hispanic white
<9	57.1%	6.5%	9.6%	2.1%
9–11	15.3%	15.5%	19.6%	7.9%
12	18.2%	42.1%	43.3%	39.9%
13–15	7.2%	25.4%	17.2%	22.4%
16+	2.2%	10.6%	10.3%	27.6%

SOURCE: Current Population Survey, matched June–September files for 1986 and 1988, tabulations by the author.

reveal tremendous progress in educational attainment among Mexican Americans educated in the post–civil rights era. Mexican Americans who entered high school after 1965 are far more likely to have graduated than those who attended high school in the 1940s, 1950s, and early 1960s. Only 38 percent of second-generation and 29 percent of third-generation Mexican American men over the age of fifty completed high school, compared with 73 percent of the non-Hispanic whites of the same age. Such figures suggest tremendous progress in educational opportunity for Mexican Americans over the last thirty years.

Nonetheless, fewer Hispanics than non-Hispanics decide to continue their education after high school. For example, barely one-third of all young Mexican American males continue their education, compared with more than half of all non-Hispanic whites; moreover, of those Mexican Americans who do attend college, only about one-third graduate from a four-year college, compared with 60 percent of the non-Hispanic whites. The number of college graduates among third-generation Mexican Americans remains fairly constant across age groups, at about 10 percent for the oldest men in this group, those fifty-one to sixty-five years old, and 12 or 13 percent among those aged twenty-five to fifty. Only among Cubans and Central and South Americans are college degrees more common: 20 percent of the Cubans twenty-five to thirty-four years old and 15 percent of comparable South and Central Americans had completed four or more years of college in 1990.[23] But in one respect Hispanic college graduates are becoming more like non-Hispanic whites. Traditionally, Hispanics, like blacks, were more likely to concentrate in fields such as education and the social sciences, which are less remunerative than the physical sciences, business, engineering, and other technical and professional fields. Recently this trend has been reversed; in 1987 (the last year for which such statistics are available), Hispanics were almost as likely as non-Hispanic whites to receive baccalaureate degrees in the natural sciences and were more likely than they to major in computer sciences and engineering.[24]

OCCUPATIONAL STATUS

Fewer Hispanic college graduates will mean fewer Hispanics in the professions and in higher-paying occupations, but this does not translate into the doomsday predictions about their achievement that advocacy organizations commonly voice. It does not mean, for example, that there will be "a permanent Hispanic underclass" of persons "stuck in poverty because of low wages and deprived of upward mobility," as one Hispanic leader suggested in a *New York Times* article.[25] It may mean, however, that Hispanics will be more likely to hold jobs as clerks in stores and banks, as secretaries and other office support personnel, as skilled workers, and as laborers. Indeed, using the standard occupational categories of the Bureau of

Labor Statistics, one finds that, among all Hispanic (foreign-
and U.S.-born) males, the percentage who are employed in
technical, sales, and administrative support is almost 15 percent, compared to about 20 percent for non-Hispanics; about
20 percent of Hispanics and non-Hispanics alike are employed in precision production, craft, and repair; and 30 percent of Hispanics, compared to 20 percent of non-Hispanics,
are employed as operators, fabricators, and laborers. Only in
the managerial and professional and the service categories
are there very large differences along ethnic lines: 11 percent
of all Hispanic males are employed in managerial or professional jobs compared with 27 percent of all non-Hispanics;
conversely, 16 percent of the Hispanic males compared with
only 9 percent of the non-Hispanic men are employed in
service jobs.[26] But these figures include large numbers of
immigrants in the Hispanic population, who are disproportionately represented in the service industry and among
laborers.

An increasing number of Hispanics are self-employed,
many in owner-operated businesses. According to the economist Timothy Bates, who has done a comprehensive study of
minority small businesses, those owned by Hispanics are more
successful than those owned by blacks. Yet Mexican business
owners, a majority of whom are immigrants, are less well educated than any other group; one-third have completed less
than twelve years of schooling. One reason why Hispanics
may be more successful than blacks in operating small businesses, according to Bates, is that they cater to a nonminority
clientele, whereas blacks operate businesses in black neighborhoods, catering to black clients. Hispanic-owned businesses are concentrated in the retail field; about one-quarter
of both Mexican and non-Mexican Hispanic firms are retail
businesses. About 10 percent of the Mexican-owned firms are
in construction.[27]

POVERTY

Despite generally encouraging economic indicators for Hispanics, poverty rates are quite high; 26 percent of all Hispanics live below the poverty line.[28] Hispanics are more than twice as likely to be living in poverty than are persons in the general population. Two factors, however, distort the poverty data: the inclusion of Puerto Ricans, who make up about 10 percent of Hispanics, one-third of whom live in poverty; and the low earnings of new immigrants. The persistence of poverty among Puerto Ricans is one of the most troubling features of the Hispanic population, dealt with in chapter 7. Soaring poverty rates among Puerto Ricans, however, are not the result of the influx of a large number of new migrants from the island who have yet to adjust to life in the United States. On the other hand, poverty among the Mexican-origin population necessarily reflects the flood of new immigrants, many of whom start off their lives in the United States poor by American standards. Unfortunately, none of the recent data on Hispanics allow us to separate Mexican immigrants from the pool of persons counted in poverty figures. (Data from the 1990 Census which will allow such analysis is not yet available.)

An exhaustive study of the 1980 census by Frank Bean and Marta Tienda, however, suggests that nativity plays an important role in poverty data, as it does in earnings data generally. Bean and Tienda estimate that the poverty rate among U.S.-born Mexican Americans was nearly 20 percent lower than that among Mexican immigrants in 1980. Their analysis of data from the 1970 census, by contrast, shows almost no difference in poverty rates between Mexican Americans and Mexican immigrants, with both groups suffering significantly greater poverty in 1970 than in 1980. This implies that while poverty was declining among immigrants and the native-born alike between 1970 and 1980, the decline was greater for Mexican Americans.[29]

THE PUBLIC POLICY IMPLICATIONS OF SUCH FINDINGS

For most Hispanics, especially those born in the United States, the last few decades have brought greater economic opportunity and social mobility. They are building solid lower-middle- and middle-class lives that include two-parent households, with a male head who works full-time and earns a wage commensurate with his education and training. Their educational level has been steadily rising, their earnings no longer reflect wide disparities with those of non-Hispanics, and their occupational distribution is coming to resemble more closely that of the general population. They are buying homes—42 percent of all Hispanics owned or were purchasing their home in 1989, including 47 percent of all Mexican Americans—and moving away from inner cities.[30] Even in areas with very high concentrations of Hispanics, like Los Angeles, the sociologist Douglas Massey reports, "segregation [is] low or moderate on all dimensions."[31] And, in what is perhaps the ultimate test of assimilation, about one-third of all U.S.-born Hispanics under the age of thirty-five are marrying non-Hispanics.[32]

In light of the data presented here, the policy prescriptions offered by many Hispanic advocacy organizations and by most politicians seem oddly out of sync. They rely too much on government programs of doubtful efficacy. For example, a report by the National Council of La Raza calls for raising the minimum wage to improve the economic status of Hispanics, despite most economists' view that increases in the minimum wage actually decrease job opportunities for low-wage workers, especially the young.[33] Another report by the

council chastises federal officials for failing to increase Hispanic participation in the Job Training Partnership Act
(JTPA), the major federal program that provides job training
and placement for the long-term unemployed. But JTPA, like
its predecessor—the Comprehensive Employment and Training Act (CETA)—has done little to solve the problem of the
poor, long-term unemployed. The council report notes that
one-quarter of the Hispanics who went through the JTPA program did not get a job when their training was complete, and
some studies suggest that one-quarter of all JTPA participants
were no longer in the jobs for which they were trained four
and a half months after they were placed in them.[34] The fact
that Hispanics are less likely than blacks to participate in such
programs—a source of major consternation for the National
Council—may simply reflect a realistic appraisal of the
programs' worth.

There are no "magic bullets" that will eliminate all disparities between Hispanics and non-Hispanics. Improving educational attainment among Hispanics—which comes closest—is
a long and complex process. It requires a change in values,
a willingness to defer gratification, among other things. The
benefits of higher education may not be immediately apparent to young Hispanics, who in fact earn more than their non-
Hispanic white peers when they enter the labor force at an
early age but lose out in the earnings competition to those
with more schooling as they become older.[35]

Some analysts suggest that affirmative action programs in
higher education might encourage more Hispanic youth to
continue their education. But Hispanic enrollment in higher
education has been rising steadily for the last two decades
(despite a fairly constant college graduation rate during the
same period), even during times of affirmative action re-
trenchment in the 1980s. What's more, many—if not most—
affirmative action programs rely on applying less rigorous
admissions standards to Hispanic and other minority stu-

dents, not on ensuring that minority students can meet the same standards as non-minority students. The result is a higher rate of attrition among Hispanics than among non-Hispanic whites, at some institutions 61 percent higher according to one analysis. Moreover, the grade-point averages of Hispanic students admitted through affirmative action programs are often lower. At the University of California at Berkeley in the academic year 1985–86, for example, only 62 percent of the Hispanic students admitted through the school's affirmative action program maintained a 2.0 grade-point average after one year, compared with 90 percent of all regularly admitted students.[36] Shortcuts to genuine educational achievement—like those of affirmative action programs that substitute lower standards—will produce only a chimera of accomplishment.

Important as education is to the progress of Hispanics in this society, Hispanics' lower achievements in this realm must be placed in some perspective. Hispanics are certainly not the first group whose educational gains have proceeded at a slow pace. Italian Americans, for example, did not achieve educational parity with other groups until 1972—nearly six decades after the peak of Italian immigration—but now they experience one of the highest rates of educational mobility of any group.[37] Groups do not all advance at precisely the same rate in this society—sometimes because of discrimination, sometimes because of other factors. As Thomas Sowell and others have pointed out, no multiethnic society in the world exhibits utopian equality of income, education, and occupational status for every one of its ethnic groups. What is important is that opportunities be made available to all persons, regardless of race or ethnicity. Ultimately, however, it will be up to individuals to take advantage of those opportunities. Increasing numbers of Hispanics are doing just that. And no government action can replace the motivation and will to succeed that propels genuine individual achievement.

CHAPTER 6

The Immigrants

Virtually no group in the United States has undergone the kind of dramatic change in the last twenty years that has seized the Hispanic population. Not only has it more than doubled in size, but it is becoming increasingly an immigrant population as well. In 1970 barely one in five Hispanics was foreign-born. Today more than one in three is; of Hispanic adults, one in two was born outside the United States. For years the debate about Hispanics has been over whether they are an indigenous minority that has suffered generations of discrimination and deprivation, like blacks, or whether they are more like immigrants of a previous era, whose poverty and deprivation were temporary. Hispanic leaders have pressed the former argument and have, by and large, convinced policy makers that Hispanics are entitled to programs and benefits aimed at redressing past discrimination. But what about Hispanic immigrants, who constitute an increasing proportion of the Hispanic population? Where do they fit in this scheme? As we saw in chapter 5, the presence of so many recent immigrants has greatly distorted evidence regarding the current achievement and progress of Hispanics. Will the continued flow of millions of immigrants threaten to undermine Hispanic achievement in the decades to come? Can we

121

really expect Latin immigrants to follow in the footsteps of their European predecessors? Or are they so different, and the conditions they encounter so changed, that their assimilation will be impossible?

HOW MANY?

In 1989 about 140,000 persons immigrated from Latin America.[1] Since 1980 about two million Latin immigrants have come to the United States legally.[2] Latins now make up about a third of all legal immigrants, as they have for nearly three decades. In addition to the quarter million legal immigrants who come to the United States from Latin America each year, an unknown number of Latin immigrants enter the country illegally. Estimates vary from fewer than 100,000 to more than 500,000 each year. Indeed, throughout the decade of the 1980s the Immigration and Naturalization Service apprehended an average of one million illegal aliens each year—but that figure includes multiple apprehensions for some individuals.[3] The best estimates of the number of Latins who immigrate illegally put it at between 100,000 and 300,000 a year—a number roughly equal to that of all legal immigrants from Latin America.[4]

Immigrants come from each of the countries of Latin America, but the most important sources of immigration in recent years have been Mexico, Cuba, the Dominican Republic, and, increasingly in the 1980s, El Salvador and Nicaragua. By far the largest number of Latin immigrants come from Mexico, more than 70,000 legal immigrants a year plus an equal or greater number of illegal aliens. Cuban immigration has been heavy, though sporadic, in recent years. In 1980 about 125,000 people fled Cuba by boat, in the largest surge of Cuban refugees since the 1960s, and about 3,000 Cubans immigrated in 1989.[5] Increasing numbers of immigrants are coming to the United States from Central America and the Dominican Republic. About 25,000 Dominicans immigrate legally each year, plus an unknown number illegally, a disproportionate number of whom are women.[6] Much of the immigration from Central America remains hidden from official statistics, because a high percentage of it is illegal. Hundreds of thousands of persons have fled El Salvador and Nicaragua over the last decade, as war and failing economies have ravaged both countries. In 1980 some 85,000 Salvadorans were counted in the U.S. census. Estimates of the Salvadoran population in the United States today range from 250,000 to nearly a million. Until recently, Central American immigrants were disproportionately from the professional class; however, the profile of the current illegal Central American immigrants more closely resembles that of Mexican illegals.

A PROFILE OF LATIN IMMIGRANTS

Stereotypes of Latin immigrants persist. Many people continue to think of them as peasants who come north seeking jobs in agriculture. The stereotype is probably a holdover from the era of the Bracero Program, which brought some 350,000 Mexican men a year to work as contract laborers in agriculture during the 1950s.[7] But the stereotype of the Latino farm worker is at best an anachronism. Not only do most immigrants today work in urban areas, but most lived in towns and cities before coming to the United States. One study of Mexican immigrants found that only a third of the immigrants' fathers lived in rural areas at the time of the immigrants' migration.[8] Nonetheless, most Latin immigrants, especially Mexicans, are poorly educated by U.S. standards and face years of substandard wages in the U.S. labor market.

Mexican immigrants, on the average, earn only about half as much as non-Hispanic whites. They have larger families and higher fertility rates than other groups do.[9] Lower earnings and larger families result in greater poverty among Hispanic immigrants, about one-third of whom live in poverty. Their educational levels are the lowest of any group in the United States. Among the youngest age group, who are the best educated, only 28 percent have completed twelve or more years of school. Nonetheless, even these poorly educated immigrants will make progress as they stay longer in the United States. The economist George Borjas estimates that Mexican immigrants will close the gap with comparable native-born workers at a rate of about 0.6 percent a year, although their earnings may never completely reach those of non-Hispanic whites.[10] Acquiring proficiency in English is a key element to improving earnings among Hispanic immigrants.[11]

Cubans are the second-largest group of foreign-born Hispanics in the United States. While Mexicans are often regarded as the proletariat of Latin immigrants, Cubans have generally been regarded as the elite. The early waves of Cuban refugees in the 1960s included large numbers of landowners, professionals, and entrepreneurs and their families, but recent Cuban immigrants have come from more modest backgrounds. Alejandro Portes and Robert Bach, authors of a six-year comparative study, interviewed over 1,400 Mexican and Cuban immigrants as they arrived in the United States in 1973–74 and again in 1976 and 1979, in one of the most comprehensive studies of its kind ever done. A majority of the Cuban men interviewed by Portes and Bach came from just four occupational categories: skilled workers (carpenters, plumbers, and so on), intermediate service workers (barbers, taxi drivers, and so on), semiskilled urban laborers, and unskilled urban laborers. The Cubans who immigrated in the mid-1970s were not particularly well educated: the median years of school completed was 8.6.[12]

The most recent Cuban refugees, known as Marielitos, after the Cuban port of Mariel, from which most of them departed by boat in 1980, are less well educated than those of earlier waves. The boat lift included significant numbers of felons and mentally ill, perhaps 5 percent of the total, who fled when Castro cynically emptied Cuban mental hospitals and jails during the mass exodus. About four thousand Marielitos are at present serving time in U.S. jails.[13] Nonetheless, within three years after their arrival in the United States, an estimated 15 percent of the Marielitos had started their own businesses and 13 percent were in professional or technical occupations, according to a study by Portes and Alex Stepick. Unlike previous Cuban refugees, the Marielitos did not receive direct government assistance. Even without it, however, most Marielitos found jobs—about one-third of them were employed by other Cubans—or were assisted by the private charity of family and friends.[14]

Central Americans, most of them from El Salvador and Nicaragua, form the third-largest group of recent Hispanic immigrants. Information about the number and the social and economic condition of the Central American immigrants is imprecise because so many are in the United States illegally, but data from the government's monthly Current Population Survey suggest that their profile is changing.[15] Persons of Central or South American origin were substantially less likely to be in a professional or managerial position and more likely to be in a service occupation in 1990 than they had been in 1980. In fact, their proportion in the professions has been declining steadily since 1960.[16] The earnings of Central and South American males in 1989 were the second-lowest of any Hispanic group, after those of Mexicans, undoubtedly reflecting the large influx of recent immigrants.

THE HISTORICAL ANALOGY

The relatively low socioeconomic status of Latin immigrants is not unusual for an immigrant group. Virtually all large immigrant groups have suffered economic deprivation and social isolation, at least during their early years in the United States. The remarkable success with which millions of Germans, Irish, Italians, Greeks, Poles, Jews, and others were absorbed into the fabric of American society sometimes blinds us to the difficulty each of these groups faced at first. Nearly every group met resistance and prejudice from natives, who were anxious to protect their own status against what they saw as incursions by foreigners. Thomas Sowell recounts an example of this in his book *Ethnic America*:

The remarkable achievements—especially intellectual achievements—of later generations of Jews cannot simply be read back into the immigrant generation. These children often had serious educational problems. A 1910 survey of a dozen cities found two-thirds of the children of Polish Jews to be below the normal grade for their age.... As late as World War I, soldiers of Russian—mostly Jewish—origin averaged among the lowest mental test scores of any of the ethnic groups tested by the U.S. Army. These results led a leading contemporary authority on tests to declare that this disproved "the popular belief that the Jew is highly intelligent." Like many confident "expert" conclusions, this one failed to stand the test of time.[17]

Nor did differences between ethnic immigrants and native-stock Americans disappear immediately. The sociologist Richard Alba reports,

In general, the attainments of men from Southern and Eastern European backgrounds (with the exception of Russians, a category that is mostly Jewish) lag behind those of men of English ancestry; so do those of men of Irish, French, and German ancestries.... But these disadvantages have largely faded for the men in the third and later generations.[18]

Some skeptics argue that inferences about Hispanic immigrants cannot be drawn from the experiences of European immigrants nearly a century ago. They claim that most Europeans arrived at a time when there was greater demand for unskilled or semiskilled labor and when all Americans were less highly educated, so immigrants were less disadvantaged relative to the native population than immigrants are today. But the educational deficit of today's Hispanic immigrants is no greater than that of immigrants in the early part of the century, many of whom had no formal education and could neither read nor write. More than half the immigrants from southern Italy at the turn of the century were illiterate, as were nearly half of those from Lithuania and about 40 percent of those from Russia, most of whom were Jews.[19] What's more, many European immigrants came from peasant backgrounds and were thrust into urban environments for which they were ill suited. Sowell notes, for example, that the Irish typically lacked the skills necessary in an urban economy.[20] Yet most Hispanic immigrants come from urban backgrounds and have worked at trades that provide them with at least rudimentary skills to find work in the United States. The best proof, perhaps, is that a high proportion of Hispanic immigrants participate in the labor force: nearly 90 percent of the males, a rate substantially higher than that for non-Hispanic whites or native-born Hispanics.

There are, however, some important differences between earlier immigrants and those who are immigrating now, the biggest being in the circumstances they encounter in the United States. Several commentators have noted that ethnic groups today become interest groups in the United States because the members of such groups frequently live together and have similar occupations.[21] But Hispanic immigrants become part of a new kind of interest group—the disadvantaged minority—whose very existence, at least with respect to Hispanics, depends on their inclusion.

HOW HISPANIC IMMIGRANTS DIFFER FROM PREVIOUS GROUPS

Most earlier immigrants to the United States were forced eventually to sever their ties to their native lands because regular travel back and forth was unfeasible. Although many European immigrants did, in fact, return permanently to their country of origin—as many as 73 percent of the Italian immigrants in some years—those who chose to remain found it more difficult to maintain ties to their homeland.[22] For a while, immigrants could keep a thriving cultural identity in their own enclaves—much as Cuban immigrants in Miami do today. As successive generations moved out of central cities to the suburbs, however, immigrant groups became less distinct from each other and from the American mainstream.

But Hispanic immigrants, especially Mexicans, live very close to their homeland. In the most extreme instances, some families along the U.S.–Mexican border operate almost as if the border did not exist. Women living in Mexican towns like Nuevo Laredo (which is separated from Laredo, Texas, by a short bridge) sometimes cross the border to give birth in American hospitals both because the health care is superior and because the child born there will be an American citizen, even though he may grow up in Mexico. The changing of residence from one side of the border to the other is often determined more by the immediate needs of the family than by any recognition of legal borders or differences in political status on either side of that border. Thus some Mexican

Americans or resident aliens may find it advantageous to leave the United States when they pass their peak earning years and return to Mexico, where pensions and social security can be stretched further. Even if Hispanics do not decide to return to Mexico, Central America, the Caribbean, or wherever they are from, they are able to make frequent visits, by car to many areas and by relatively inexpensive air travel to others. Family ties between those who have immigrated and those who have remained behind are much stronger today than they were in previous eras of immigration by other ethnic groups. Proximity permits Hispanics to maintain their distinct culture and language to a far greater degree than other immigrants could in the past. Moreover, Spanish-language radio and television, which reports much Latin American news, allows Latin immigrants to keep up with events in their country of origin.

Another important difference is that large-scale immigration from southern and eastern Europe declined significantly after the passage of the 1924 National Origins Act, which greatly restricted the number of immigrants from those regions.[23] Immigration from Latin America, on the other hand, has been constant, accounting for about one-third of all legal immigration since at least 1955. Richard Lamm, who favors restricting immigration from Latin America, says, "The migration stream of the 1910s would not have been assimilated had it continued unabated, had it been augmented by decades of followers."[24] The implication, of course, is that in order for Latin immigrants to be absorbed successfully today, Latin immigration must cease. That is not likely to happen, even if political circumstances favored it, which they don't. The border with Mexico is simply too long and too porous to prevent persons who want to come to the United States from doing so. As long as the income gap between the two countries remains large—it is now the greatest found between any two contiguous countries in the world—people will continue to take great risks to come here from Mexico.[25] Efforts to curtail legal immigration from Latin America would simply result in larger numbers of illegal aliens, who would be even less likely to be assimilated. To date, no measures have proved effective in stopping the flow of illegal aliens from Latin America. Indeed, the Immigration Reform and Control Act of 1986 (IRCA), which for the first time prohibited U.S. employers from hiring illegal aliens, has done little to curb illegal immigration.[26]

NATURALIZATION OF LATIN IMMIGRANTS

Although the overwhelming majority of Latins who immigrate legally indicate they intend to live permanently in the United States, most never become American citizens. Naturalization rates, however, are not uniformly low among all Latin immigrant groups. By far the lowest naturalization rate occurs among Mexican immigrants. In 1989 only 13 percent of all Mexican immigrants admitted since the previous decade (after 1970) had naturalized. (Mexican immigrants, however, did not have the very lowest rates, for only 11 percent of all Canadian immigrants in the cohort had naturalized by 1989.) Other large Latin immigrant populations had naturalized at somewhat higher rates: 31.5 percent of the Colombians, 27 percent of the Cubans, and 20 percent of the Dominicans.[27] Latin immigrants also tend to delay naturalization longer than other groups. Half of all Mexican immigrants who become citizens have lived in the United States twelve or more years prior to naturalization.[28] Since a majority of the Mexicans admitted legally have spent at least one year in the United States before their legal admission, the period of U.S. residency before naturalization is probably even longer than it appears.

The clearest explanation for low naturalization rates among Mexicans is their proximity to their native land (which may also explain why so few Canadian immigrants become U.S. citizens). But other factors, too, may be at work. The low educational attainment of Mexican immigrants, some researchers suggest, plays a role, as does their perception that U.S. citizenship would not provide them with added privileges or benefits.[29]

Some Hispanic organizations have begun to show concern about the low naturalization rates of Latin immigrants. The National Association of Latino Elected and Appointed Officials (NALEO) started work in 1985 on a project to increase citizenship among Latin immigrants. In a survey of Latin immigrants, NALEO found that while virtually all Latin immigrants (98 percent of those interviewed) planned to live permanently in the United States, nearly half (46 percent) believed there were no real benefits to becoming a U.S. citizen.[30] Only about a third of the immigrants interviewed had actually become citizens, although more than half had taken some steps toward eligibility for citizenship, such as studying English or U.S. history.

PUSHING THE LIMITS

As the Hispanic population in the United States is increasingly composed of Latin immigrants and their U.S.-born children, the idea that Hispanics should be treated like a permanently disadvantaged, indigenous minority group makes little sense. Programs created to overcome the effects of past discrimination—affirmative action in employment and education, for example—were clearly never intended to benefit immigrants. As two Hispanic academics, Rodolfo de la Garza and Armando Trujillo, put it recently,

While there is no doubt that immigrants should enjoy all Constitutional guarantees, it is unreasonable to suggest that immigrants should be favored over citizens. That, however, appears to be the unintended consequence of the convergence of high immigration and policies such as affirmative action and new language policies produced by the civil rights movement.[31]

The debate over policies that are perceived to favor immigrants at the expense of the native-born is nowhere fiercer than in the effort to extend rights and benefits to persons who are in the United States illegally. A controversial Supreme Court ruling in 1982 (*Plyler* v. *Doe*), for example, required states to provide free public education to the children of illegal aliens.[32] The case stemmed from a Texas law that allowed school districts to charge tuition to illegal aliens whose children attended public schools. Texas argued that the state should not be required to provide free public services to persons who had no legal right to be in the state. In a 5-to-4 ruling, the Court rejected Texas's argument and said that minor children of illegal aliens were entitled to free public education under the equal-protection clause of the Fourteenth Amendment. Justice Thurgood Marshall's concurring opinion argued that to deny such children the benefits of a free public education would no doubt cost society more in the long run, by making it likely that such children would grow up to be dependent on welfare. The logic of the argument, however, may not have been persuasive to state officials who seem faced with a Hobson's choice: pay now or later for services to persons who have no right to be in the United States in the first place. It probably heightened the frustration of state officials that these children required additional special services, especially language instruction.

Emboldened by success in securing the right to free public education for the children of illegal aliens, Hispanic organizations have made other gains as well. Illegal aliens in Texas won the right to unemployment compensation in a case filed by Texas Rural Legal Aid; and in California, the Mexican

American Legal Defense and Education Fund (MALDEF) won a suit preventing the state from charging illegal aliens higher tuition fees than it charges legal state residents.[33] But the most egregious suits to date have been those which would extend to illegal aliens the right to participate in the electoral process.

In 1982 the U.S. attorney in San Francisco began an investigation of alleged election fraud involving community voter registration projects in nine northern California counties. When lists of newly registered voters who had requested bilingual ballots in the 1982 election were matched against lists of legal aliens, a number of noncitizens were found to have voted. Further checks revealed that not only legal resident aliens were voting in the election but also a number of persons who were in the country illegally. The American Civil Liberties Union filed suit against the U.S. attorney on behalf of a naturalized citizen who claimed that the investigation had a chilling effect on voter participation of persons like himself who were indeed entitled to vote. An eleven-member panel of the Ninth Circuit Court of Appeals upheld the plaintiff's claim, reversing a lower-court ruling that declined to interfere in the federal prosecutor's investigation.[34] The Supreme Court vacated the decision as moot because the U.S. attorney stopped the investigation.

Illegal aliens have no legal right to vote in elections, the Ninth Circuit Court opinion notwithstanding, but some Hispanic leaders have begun to call for an extension of the franchise to noncitizens. Jose Angel Gutierrez, the founder of La Raza Unida party (see chapter 3) and now an attorney in Dallas, recently told a cheering audience of local Hispanic activists that "resident aliens ought to be entitled to vote *ya, pronto....* "[35] The former president and general counsel of MALDEF, Joaquin Avila, also recently called for allowing noncitizens to vote in U.S. elections.[36] Even without the right to vote, however, illegal aliens can affect the outcome of elections because their presence is being used to create majority Hispanic electoral districts (see chapter 2).

Such policies clearly go beyond the guarantee of equal protection of the laws. Hispanic organizations that insist on special benefits, not just for Hispanic citizens but for immigrants as well—legal and illegal—severely strain the comity of the American public. Moreover, there is no reason to believe that the Latin immigrants who are the purported beneficiaries of such policies seek their implementation. Hundreds of thousands of Latin immigrants come to the United States each year to work—not to collect welfare payments or unemployment compensation, not to participate in affirmative action programs or swell the voter rolls for ethnic politicians. But if Hispanic organizations continue to insist that millions of newcomers be awarded special status once here, they may find the doors closing to future Latin immigrants.

IMMIGRANTS AS INTEREST GROUP

Without the presence of millions of low-skilled immigrants—many of whom live in poverty, at least temporarily—the Hispanic profile would be substantially different from what it is. Earnings differentials between Hispanics and non-Hispanics would be significantly smaller. In my own calculations of earnings data on the Mexican-origin population, for example, the gap in earnings between non-Hispanic white males and Mexican-origin males is cut almost in half when Mexican immigrants are taken out of the equation. In general, if it were not for the presence of so many new immigrants in the pot, the assimilation process for Hispanics would appear far more advanced than it does. Studies of language shift among Hispanics, for example, show that virtually all native-born Hispanics are fluent in English and that, by the third generation, more than half of the native-born Hispanics speak only English.[37] Were it not for Hispanic immigrants, the much vaunted Hispanic school dropout problem would be much diminished: native-born Hispanics would be graduating from high school at rates only about 10 percent lower than those for non-Hispanic whites, not 40–50 percent lower, as many analysts claim. Hispanic immigrants—especially Mexicans and Central Americans, whose low skills and poor education guarantee slow progress up the economic ladder—are a vital component of the Hispanic claim to compensatory programs and affirmative action. Without them, Hispanic leaders would have a much more difficult time persuading the public that Hispanics are a permanently disadvantaged group.

In the post–affirmative action era, the relationship between new immigrants and the members of their own ethnic group who have lived in the United States longer and have already begun to assimilate is turned on its head. In the past, the members of the older ethnic community saw it as their duty to help newcomers adjust to American life. No doubt some of this concern was motivated by fear that the new immigrants would jeopardize the hard-won social standing of the earlier group; whatever its source, the concern manifested itself in efforts to help new immigrants. Sowell notes that "the Eastern European Jews were an acute embarrassment to the German Jews in America. . . . Overriding all of these antipathies, however, was the Jewish philanthropic tradition. German-Jewish organizations made strenuous efforts to aid, and especially to Americanize, the Eastern European Jewish immigrants."[38] Few such efforts are taking place in the Hispanic community. With the exception of the NALEO immigration project, no major Hispanic effort exists to help Hispanic immigrants learn English or encourage naturalization.

When I was president of U.S. English, I frequently reminded other Hispanic leaders whom I debated that U.S. English was spending more than $100,000 a year on a project

to teach English to new immigrants while their organizations were spending nothing. None of these leaders ever
offered to explain why their organizations do so little to
help Hispanic newcomers. One explanation may be that without so many poor and unassimilated Hispanic immigrants,
the rationale for many of the programs these Hispanic leaders favor disappears. Of course, Hispanic organizations do
lobby for government programs for Hispanic immigrants,
but the thrust of these programs is hardly assimilationist.
More important, as de la Garza and Trujillo have suggested,
Hispanic organizations are reluctant to admit that the programs for which they lobby are really aimed at immigrants.
Bilingual ballots, for example, are promoted on the theory
that significant numbers of native-born Hispanics cannot
read an English ballot; bilingual education is promoted
on the theory that indigenous Hispanics have the right to
maintain their ancestral language and culture. Yet without
the constant influx of Spanish-speaking immigrants the
need for such programs would evaporate within one generation.

In the current era, assimilation for Hispanic immigrants
appears to mean adopting the ethos of entitlement. Borjas
and other commentators note, for example, that welfare rates
for Hispanic immigrants increase the longer they reside in
the United States.[39] "It is ironic that an assimilation process
that improves immigrant earnings and employment opportunities also seems to increase their propensities to enter the
welfare system," says Borjas.[40] Then too, immigrants are not
reluctant to take advantage of programs like affirmative action, which were originally intended to redress discrimination against indigenous minorities. Cuban immigrants, for
example, are eligible for federal minority business set-asides
and other affirmative action programs, despite their relative
affluence.

WHAT THE FUTURE HOLDS

It is too early to tell whether the most recent wave of Hispanic immigrants will be assimilated as others were before them. Certainly, there are some economic grounds for optimism. Immigrants' earnings increase the longer they are in the United States; and some economists, most notably Barry Chiswick, maintain that they eventually surpass those of native-born Hispanics.[41] Others, like George Borjas, believe that the lifetime earnings of Hispanic immigrants will be lower than those of native-born Hispanics, but not by much. Borjas estimates that the most recent Mexican immigrants will earn about 14.5 percent less than Mexican Americans over their lifetime.[42] Nonetheless, Hispanic immigrants are moving up the economic ladder. A surprising number of Latin immigrants own their home—56 percent of all Mexican immigrants and 63 percent of all Cubans.[43] And the longer Hispanic immigrants reside in the United States, the less likely they are to be concentrated in barrios or other ethnic enclaves. An Urban Institute study found, for example, that Hispanic immigrants living in Los Angeles in 1980 who had immigrated twenty years earlier experienced fairly low levels of isolation from non-Hispanic whites; the longer the immigrants lived in the United States, the less likely they were to be ethnically isolated.[44] The demographer Douglas Massey has found similar results: immigrants are often likely to be highly segregated in inner cities when they first arrive; but as their economic status improves, they move to more integrated suburban areas.[45]

Of course, illegal aliens fare less well than immigrants who have been lawfully admitted.[46] According to the General Accounting Office, which reviewed wage data from several studies of illegal aliens, such workers earn from 130 to 200 percent of the minimum wage, on the average. In areas with a high concentration of illegal aliens, wages were lower than in areas where few immigrants resided.[47]

Given the likelihood that even this generation of low-skilled immigrants will make progress in this society, the rationale for treating Hispanics as permanently disadvantaged may be running out. At some point, policy makers are bound to recognize that there are important differences between the native-born Hispanic population and Hispanic immigrants. When they do, Hispanic leaders may find it more difficult to base their claim to civil rights entitlements on the backs of immigrants, whose poverty is temporary and for whom this society offers greater opportunity and equity than they could dream of obtaining in their homeland.

CHAPTER 7

The Puerto Rican Exception

There is much reason for optimism about the progress of Hispanics in the United States. Cuban immigrants have achieved social and economic parity with other Americans in one generation. Cuban Americans differ little from other Americans in earnings or education, being well represented in professional and business occupations and among other high-wage earners. Mexican Americans, the oldest and largest Hispanic group, are moving steadily into the middle class, with the majority having established solid, working- and middle-class lives. Even Mexican immigrants and those from other Latin American countries, many of whom have very little formal education, appear to be largely self-sufficient. The vast majority of such immigrants—two-thirds—live above the poverty line, having achieved a standard of living far above that attainable by them in their countries of origin.

There is no indication that any of these groups is in danger of becoming a permanent underclass. If Hispanics choose to (and most *are* choosing to), they will quickly join the mainstream of this society. As their economic status improves, most will opt to move out of ethnic enclaves and live among those who share the same social status regardless of ethnic background. Many will intermarry; already half of all Mexican

Americans in California choose non-Hispanic spouses.[1] In other words, the evidence suggests that Hispanics, by and large, are behaving much as other ethnic groups did in the past. One group of Hispanics, however, appears not to be following this pattern. Puerto Ricans occupy the lowest rung of the social and economic ladder among Hispanics, and a disturbing number of them show little hope of climbing higher.

In 1961, in their influential book *Beyond the Melting Pot*, Nathan Glazer and Daniel P. Moynihan described Puerto Ricans "adapting to a city [New York] very different from the one to which earlier immigrant groups adapted, and . . . being modified by the new process of adaptation in new and hardly predictable ways."[2] Thirty years later the results of that adaptation are apparent. Puerto Ricans are not simply the poorest of all Hispanic groups; they experience the highest degree of social dysfunction of any Hispanic group and exceed that of blacks on some indicators. Thirty-nine percent of all Puerto Rican families are headed by single women; 53 percent of all Puerto Rican children are born out of wedlock; the proportion of men in the labor force is lower among Puerto Ricans than any other group, including blacks; Puerto Ricans have the highest welfare participation rate of any group in New York, where nearly half of all Puerto Ricans in the United States live. Yet, on the average, Puerto Ricans are better educated than Mexicans and nearly as well educated as Cubans, with a median education of twelve years.[3] Why are Puerto Ricans faring so poorly in the United States? And what lessons can be learned from their experience?

ISLAND ROOTS

As the sociologist Clara Rodriguez trumpets in the title of her book *Puerto Ricans: Born in the U.S.A.*, Puerto Ricans are Americans by birth. Puerto Rico was acquired by the United States from Spain at the conclusion of the Spanish-American War in 1898; after passage of the Jones Act in 1917, all Puerto Ricans became U.S. citizens, whether born on the island or in the States. But U.S. citizenship initially had little direct bearing on those living on the island. They continued to speak Spanish, to work primarily in agriculture—mostly on sugar-cane farms—and to live at subsistence levels. Moreover, until 1947, they had little political autonomy. Puerto Ricans elected their first governor in 1949, Luis Muñoz Marin; they cannot vote for president, although both major parties do grant Puerto Rican delegates voting rights at presidential nominating conventions; and Puerto Rico is represented in Congress by a nonvoting member of Congress.

Conditions on the island, while better than those in most other Caribbean nations, were far from ideal. The first large waves of Puerto Rican migrants left the island in the 1920s to settle as far away as Hawaii, where they worked on sugar plantations. Migration to the mainland increased significantly in the 1940s and 1950s. Service in both World War II and the Korean War introduced many young Puerto Rican men (more than 100,000) to the world beyond their island home and prompted many to leave in search of greater economic opportunity. The low airfare from the island to New York, which was about $50 one-way in the 1950s and today is only about $175, made leaving feasible. Once the first migrants were established, the stream of migrants to the mainland grew steadily. There are about two-thirds as many Puerto Ricans living in the United States (2.2 million) as there on the island (3.6 million); and second- and third-generation mainland-born Puerto Ricans now account for a majority of the total Puerto Rican population of New York, still the largest Puerto Rican population center anywhere.

The decision of so many Puerto Ricans to settle in New York City and the surrounding areas was a fateful one. Initially, the city provided ready access to jobs that required few skills, many in the garment industry, which employed large numbers of Puerto Rican women. Although the number of jobs in New York City remained stable during the 1950s and 1960s, the city lost nearly 40 percent of its manufacturing jobs in that period. Industrial and manufacturing workers from many parts of the Northeast left in search of work in the Sunbelt or in the West or found jobs in the area's burgeoning service industry. But Puerto Rican families, by and large, chose to stay, and many ended up on welfare. By 1960 half of all Puerto Rican families were already receiving some form of public assistance.[4] The fact that so many Puerto Ricans were eligible for welfare reflected another aspect of their life in the United States: their growing propensity to form families without benefit of marriage—a tradition with roots on the island but which has transmogrified into welfare dependency in the United States.

FEMALE-HEADED HOUSEHOLDS

Civil or religious marriage has traditionally been less common among poor Puerto Ricans than among other Hispanics, on the island as well as in the United States. As late as 1950 one-quarter of all unions in Puerto Rico were consensual or common law.[5] According to Joseph P. Fitzpatrick, author of *Puerto Rican Americans*, the children born to such unions were recognized in Puerto Rico as "natural" children, products of a stable, though not legally married, couple.[6] By tradition, fathers of such children were expected to provide for their welfare and for the welfare of the mother and any other children she might have from previous unions, so long as the man lived in the home. He might also bring into the home children from another consensual union or marriage that had dissolved. This practice continued in New York. Fitzpatrick notes, "This is not an uncommon phenomenon among Puerto Rican families. New Yorkers have complained about the difficulty of understanding the differing names of children in some Puerto Rican households. . . . If a visitor asks a boy if the girl with him is his sister, he may respond, 'Yes, on my father's side,' or 'Yes, on my mother's side.' "[7]

The "adaptation process" about which Glazer and Moynihan wrote, however, saw many Puerto Rican fathers abandoning responsibility for their children to the state. This was made relatively easier in New York, where welfare was both readily available and provided the nation's most generous benefits. As L. H. Gann and Peter Duignan observe in their book *The Hispanics in the United States*, Puerto Ricans were "the first immigrant group who unwittingly moved into what became . . . a welfare economy with a powerful and intrusive bureaucracy, a high level of public expenditure, and a strong commitment to social planning."[8] In 1977, Hispanics accounted for 42 percent of all recipients of Aid to Families with Dependent Children (AFDC) in New York City; by 1986, they constituted 54 percent of the AFDC caseload, even though Puerto Ricans make up only about 12 percent of the city's population.[9] Welfare recipience has risen so steeply and is now on so high a level that the state Department of Social Services recently conducted its own survey of public assistance and food stamp recipients to better understand the nature of Hispanic welfare dependency. The department's report, titled "Hispanic ADC Recipients in New York City: Prospects for Employment and Self-Sufficiency," offered little hope on either count.[10]

The results of the department's survey, published in 1990, confirm a disturbing pattern of long-term welfare dependency by families headed by Puerto Rican women. (Less than 5 percent of the Hispanic AFDC recipients were men, who must be unable to work in order to qualify.) The majority of the Puerto Rican recipients were women who had never been married; 57 percent had had their first child before they were twenty years old. Less than 60 percent of the Puerto Rican recipients had ever held a job, and less than 20 percent had worked within the previous three years.[11] More than one-third of all Puerto Rican recipients had been on welfare continuously for more than ten years. Puerto Rican recipients averaged ninety-five months on public assistance—more than seven and one-half years, the longest average duration of any group receiving public assistance. Perhaps most telling, 41 percent of the Puerto Rican women on welfare were second-generation participants; one or both parents had received some form of public assistance as well.[12]

Although Puerto Rican welfare recipients were, in general, poorly educated (nearly one-third had completed less than nine years of schooling), deficient job skills alone do not explain why so few Puerto Rican women worked. Puerto Ricans differed most from other welfare recipients in their attitudes toward work and family, which were markedly different from black recipients'. Nearly 60 percent of the Puerto Rican women cited family reasons for their failure to work. Puerto Rican women were less likely than black women to be willing to place their children in day care, even if doing so would enable them to earn enough to support their families without welfare; 54 percent of the Puerto Rican women, compared with only about 17 percent of the black women, said they would be afraid to leave their children in day care or after-school care in order to take a job.[13]

The Puerto Rican women in the Department of Social Services study showed surprisingly strong family attachment and traditional family values. What they lacked was a strong work ethic, at least with regard to work outside the home. Indeed, Puerto Rican women have the lowest labor force participation rates of any group—41 percent, a figure that has varied little in the past three decades despite rising participation rates by women generally during that period. Many of these women indicated they believed that their primary obligation was to care for their children and that the material needs of the family should be met by someone else. Nearly half said they believed that mothers of school-age children should not work outside the home; 41 percent said that welfare provided better for their families than they could themselves, whereas only 14 percent of the black recipients voiced similar views.[14] These findings offer little promise that welfare reform efforts such as the 1988 Family Support Act, which mandates job training and child care programs, will be successful in moving Puerto Rican women off welfare.

In a traditional Puerto Rican family, the family's financial needs would be met by the children's father, even when the father was not married to the mother. Increasingly, however, the material needs of poor families are met by the state, which provides subsidized housing, food stamps, medical care, and cash assistance to families whose poverty entitles them to such benefits. Whether the availability of such benefits actively promotes family breakup is a contentious issue, but at the very least, as Fitzpatrick notes, welfare provides women unhappy in their relationships the economic security to terminate them. Fitzpatrick warns, however, "The welfare check is hardly a substitute for the brother, cousin, *compadre* [godparent], or friend in the working out of elemental loyalties which keep men and women aware of the bonds that link them in a common struggle for survival and achievement."[15] Adequate substitute or not, welfare has supplanted the family network of support for much of New York's Puerto Rican community.

FAMILY STABILITY AND
PUERTO RICAN ACHIEVEMENT

The relationship between the breakdown of the family and diminished Puerto Rican achievement is perhaps best illustrated by its converse: where the family is strong and intact, achievement is high. Fewer Puerto Rican families consist of married couples (57 percent, compared with 80 percent among whites and 72 percent among Mexican Americans), but Puerto Rican married-couple families exhibit the same intergenerational progress usually associated with immigrants and their children.[16] A small study of intact Puerto Rican families conducted by Fordham University in the mid-1970s found the adult children of such families performing well above the norm on every indicator.[17] Yet their parents were typical of Puerto Ricans of the generation that migrated to the United States on almost all indicators except one: the parents had formed and maintained intact families. These adult children of intact Puerto Rican families had a median education of 12.4 years, and nearly 20 percent of them had completed college. By comparison, nationwide only about 4 percent of the Puerto Ricans had completed four or more years of college in 1975, and the median education for Puerto Ricans was 10.3 years.[18] Nearly 40 percent of the child generation worked as professionals or managers, and about equal numbers held clerical, sales, or craft jobs. Only 20 percent were operatives, laborers, or in service jobs.[19] Again, their contemporaries showed a very different occupational distribution, with only about 15 percent employed as professionals or managers, and more than half as laborers, operatives, or workers in the service industry.[20]

The families in the Fordham study suggest that the ability to maintain an intact family confers considerable social and economic benefits to parents and their children. The Puerto Rican families in the Fordham parent generation did not differ from other Puerto Ricans who migrated to New York City. Like most Puerto Rican migrants, the men and women in the parent generation were somewhat better educated than their own parents but poorly educated by mainland standards. Parents experienced difficulty with English, with 20 percent being unable to write English and 10 percent unable to read it, even after having lived in the United States for three decades. And, of course, they encountered the same economic conditions faced by other Puerto Ricans who migrated in the 1940s and 1950s, including the loss of available jobs in manufacturing, which is frequently cited as a prime factor contributing to high welfare dependency of Puerto Rican women and the low labor force participation of Puerto Rican men. Yet this group of Puerto Rican families provided a stable, nurturing environment for their children, whose dramatic social and economic progress is atypical of Puerto Ricans.

Some social theorists contend that the poor economic prospects of black and Puerto Rican men make them less attractive prospective spouses, thus increasing the likelihood that black and Puerto Rican women will choose not to marry the fathers of their children but form female-headed households instead. It is just as likely, perhaps more so, that lower marriage rates among black and Puerto Rican males depress their work effort. June O'Neill and other economists have demonstrated that the earnings of married men are substantially higher than those of unmarried men, regardless of race. In fact, white males who are married earn an average of 20 percent more than those who remain single.[21] In the tradition-bound Puerto Rican culture, husbands are expected to take care of the material needs of their families. The families of both generations in the Fordham study said they believed that marital fulfillment required that the husband be a good provider.[22] The expectation that the husband be the primary—and in most cases sole—wage earner would seem to favor greater work effort on the part of Puerto Rican men who choose to marry. In general, poverty rates are substantially lower among married couples; and among those in which the head of the family works full-time, the poverty rate for Hispanics is only 8.5 percent.[23]

SOME HOPEFUL SIGNS

Despite the overall poor performance of Puerto Ricans, there are some bright spots in their achievement—which make their poverty seem all the more stark. While the median family earnings of Puerto Ricans are the lowest of any Hispanic groups, *individual* earnings of both male and female Puerto Ricans are actually higher than those of any other Hispanic subgroup except Cubans.[24] In 1989 Puerto Rican men had median earnings that were 82 percent of those of non-Hispanics; Puerto Rican women's median earnings were actually higher than those of non-Hispanic women.[25] Moreover, the occupational distribution of Puerto Ricans shows that substantial numbers work in white-collar jobs: nearly one-third of the Puerto Rican males who are employed work in managerial, professional, technical, sales, or administrative support jobs and more than two-thirds of the Puerto Rican females who work hold such jobs.

Moreover, Puerto Ricans are not doing uniformly poorly in all parts of the country. Those in Florida, Texas, and California, for example, perform far better than those in New York. In Texas, Clara Rodriguez notes, Puerto Ricans have a higher labor force participation rate, occupational status, college graduation rate, and per capita income than Mexicans.[26] Some analysts hypothesize that the most enterprising Puerto Ricans left New York during the economic downturn. For instance, Fitzpatrick describes the Puerto Rican settlement in Lorraine, Ohio, which was one of the most stable and successful Puerto Rican communities in the nation: by 1970 some 55 percent of the Puerto Ricans in Lorraine owned their home, and median family income among Puerto Ricans was the second-highest in the country (San Francisco boasted the highest).[27] The unmistakable conclusion is that the adaptation process for Puerto Ricans in New York was very different

from what it was elsewhere and had devastating consequences.

LABOR FORCE PARTICIPATION

Puerto Ricans appear to be the one Hispanic group that truly
fits the model of a permanently disadvantaged group, indeed
one that is developing a sizable underclass. But, according to
a recent survey of Hispanic leaders conducted by the National Council of La Raza, Puerto Rican leaders are quick to
blame poverty in their community on "cut-backs in social programs," "the Reagan budget cuts," "the lack of educational
opportunities," "the loss of jobs," and "the lack of support
systems for newcomers."[28] Not surprisingly, their recommen-
dations for eliminating poverty include more programs to
provide education and housing and more government spending to create jobs.[29] Not one of the leaders mentioned family
dissolution or low work effort as chiefly responsible for the
burgeoning Puerto Rican poverty, or suggested that too much
reliance on government—not too little government help—
might be the problem in the first place. One leader did suggest that raising Puerto Ricans' self-esteem might help; but
self-esteem is inextricably linked to achievement—the cart
can't come before the horse.

In fact, as their earnings attest, Puerto Ricans who hold
jobs are not doing appreciably worse than other Hispanics,
or non-Hispanics, once their lower educational attainment is
taken into account.[30] The low overall achievement of Puerto
Ricans is simply not attributable to the characteristics of those
who work but is a factor of the large number of those—male
and female—who are neither working nor looking for work.
Even though unemployment is higher among Puerto Ricans
than among the general population—8.6 percent, compared

with 5.3 percent for non-Hispanics in 1990—unemployment alone does not account for the large number of nonworking Puerto Ricans. Some 31 percent of all Puerto Rican males over sixteen years of age are not in the labor force at all, nor are 59 percent of all Puerto Rican females. Some of these persons are in school, but a great many more are dependent on family members or the state, or are in institutions. The incarceration rate of Puerto Rican males is disturbingly high; nearly 20,000 Hispanic men in their twenties are in criminal custody in New York State, more than are enrolled in colleges in the state.[31]

The usual explanation of why so few Puerto Ricans in New York are in the labor force is that suitable jobs are not available. Analysts like Clara Rodriguez note that Puerto Ricans traditionally worked in manufacturing jobs that were lost in the 1960s and 1970s, particularly in the garment industry. But this does not explain why Puerto Ricans did not move to fill jobs in the service industry, which were growing at a rate equal to that of the decline in manufacturing and many of which require minimal skills. Nor does it explain why Dominicans, Mexicans, and other low-skilled immigrants continue to find jobs in New York City. Indeed, the experience of Dominicans offers an interesting contrast to that of Puerto Ricans.

THE DOMINICANS IN NEW YORK

The available data suggest that Dominicans are faring better than Puerto Ricans. About half a million Dominicans have arrived in the United States since 1965, and they make up an estimated 40 percent of New York's Hispanic population. In 1980 only 30 percent of all adult Dominicans had completed high school. Yet 70 percent of all Hispanic small businesses in New York are now owned by Dominicans. And the average income of Dominicans is approximately 30 percent higher than that of Puerto Ricans.[32] Dominican men have a significantly higher labor force participation rate than Puerto Ricans; in 1980 it was 82.5 percent. Even among Dominican women who are on welfare, comparisons with Puerto Ricans show important differences. Dominican women are more likely than Puerto Ricans to have worked within the previous three years and, in fact, ever to have worked—81 percent, compared with 59 percent.[33] Dominican women on welfare are also more likely than Puerto Ricans ever to have been married—76 percent, compared with only 49 percent. Nonetheless, many Dominican households are headed by women, 37 percent. The large number of female-headed households among Dominicans in the United States is due partly to the greater number of women who immigrate from the Dominican Republic: 60 percent of all Dominican immigrants are women.[34]

The welfare dependency of Dominicans, like that of Mexican immigrants, is—ironically—a by-product of assimilation (see chapter 6). Dominican and Mexican immigrants are not immediately eligible for welfare, as their Puerto Rican counterparts, who are U.S. citizens, are; nor are they as well socialized to the welfare state. They have no alternative but to work to provide for themselves and their families. But Puerto Ricans are well versed in public assistance, in Puerto Rico as well as in the United States. About 70 percent of all persons living in Puerto Rico receive some form of government assistance; more than 50 percent qualify for food stamps (although they receive such assistance in cash).[35]

MEAN STREETS

What should be an advantage for Puerto Ricans—namely, citizenship—has turned into a liability in the welfare state.

They have been smothered by entitlements, which should serve as a warning to other Hispanics. Paradoxically, the Mexican immigrant, even the illegal alien, who comes to East Los Angeles to work in a low-skilled job has a better chance of improving his economic condition and ensuring a better legacy for his children than the Puerto Rican born in New York City who ends up on welfare does.

Parts of New York's Puerto Rican community, especially in the South Bronx, seem gripped by spiritual as well as material poverty. On a recent visit through Hispanic neighborhoods in Manhattan and the surrounding boroughs, the difference between the South Bronx and the other areas where Hispanics live was palpable. The residents of East Harlem, Washington Heights, and other Hispanic areas of the city were clearly mostly poor and working-class people—some Puerto Ricans, but mainly Dominicans, Colombians, Cubans, and Mexicans.[36] The vibrant commercial areas, even the manner in which the people moved on the street, attested to the vitality of the neighborhoods. By contrast, the streets of the South Bronx were filled with men and women whose bearing suggested they had no place to go. Men stood in groups in vacant lots; women with baby carriages and toddlers in tow strolled slowly, aimlessly down the street; the only commerce visible was that of the open-air drug markets. Unlike the working poor, these members of the urban underclass have little chance of improving their circumstances.

PUERTO RICANS AND RACE

Invariably, comparisons between Puerto Ricans and other Hispanics raise questions about what role racism plays in explaining why Puerto Ricans do more poorly. In her study of Puerto Ricans in the United States, Rodriguez suggests that racial discrimination prevents Puerto Ricans from obtaining decent jobs: "The discrimination and racism they met came as a double shock. This was especially difficult for a people unfamiliar with the sharp-edged discrimination of the United States—discrimination that actually limited life chances. What Puerto Ricans found in the labor market was different from what earlier European immigrant groups had found."[37] Rodriguez understates the prejudice and discrimination faced by earlier immigrants, who thrived despite such prejudice, and overstates the effect of employment discrimination against Puerto Ricans. Other Hispanic groups who share Puerto Ricans' mixed racial background, most notably Dominicans, face the same labor market conditions and yet manage to find jobs and retain a far higher degree of labor market attachment; this is so even among women who are single heads of households.

But if discrimination does not explain Puerto Ricans' lower social and economic status, race does play a significant role in their identity in the United States. While most Hispanics are of mixed background, the spectrum runs from white to Indian. Among Caribbean Hispanics, however, the spectrum ranges from white to black. Intermarriage between Spanish colonists and the indigenous people of the region was common, producing a *mestizo* population in areas of Hispanic settlement. In the case of Puerto Rico, the Tainos, who inhabited the island when Ponce de León established the first colony, quickly died out, the victims of mistreatment and diseases introduced by the Spanish. African slaves were brought to Puerto Rico in large numbers beginning in 1511, and slavery remained a part of the Puerto Rican economy until 1873, when it was abolished. Sexual union and intermarriage between blacks and whites in Puerto Rico produced a racially mixed people. Americans tend to view race in strictly black/white terms, but Puerto Ricans and other Caribbean Hispan-

ics make more subtle distinctions, using various words to describe people of mixed race—*trigueño*, *moreno*, and *mulatto*,
among them.

Rodriguez and other commentators claim that race and
color are not as important in Puerto Rico as they are in the
United States. This view is somewhat romanticized, however.
While it is true that intermarriage is common, Puerto Rican
society is far from color-blind, and color is closely associated
with class. Interracial unions are far more common among
the poor than among the upper class, whose features and
coloring remain distinctly European. Although Puerto Ricans
do not see race in the same dichotomous black/white terms
as other Americans do, the issue is still a sensitive one with
most Puerto Ricans. The Census Bureau, for example, is forbidden to ask the race of respondents in Puerto Rico. On the
mainland, Puerto Ricans are more likely than other Hispanics
to define themselves as nonwhite.

When Puerto Ricans of mixed race come to the United
States, they encounter different attitudes toward race, and
their own sense of racial identification may indeed change
the longer they live in the United States, with the darkest
Puerto Ricans coming to identify with American blacks over
time. According to Fitzpatrick and others who have studied
the Puerto Rican community extensively, Puerto Ricans have
traditionally made clear distinctions between American blacks
and dark-skinned Puerto Ricans, whom they refer to as *de
color* and who constitute less than 5 percent of all Puerto Ricans. In fact, tension between American blacks and Puerto
Ricans has historically been high. But Puerto Rican attitudes
toward race are not generally shared by white Americans, who
insist on categorizing all dark-skinned Puerto Ricans as black,
even though most are actually of mixed racial background.
Moreover, residential segregation of blacks remains prevalent
in the United States and affects many mixed race Puerto Ricans as well. The University of Chicago researchers Nancy

Denton and Douglas Massey, in a study of residential segregation among Caribbean Hispanics, point out, "Although
people of Spanish [mixed] race may be accepted by white
Hispanics, however, they are not accepted by Anglos, who
view them as blacks, and maintain a high degree of segregation from them. Black Hispanics, in contrast, are not accepted
as neighbors by any group except American blacks, and in
spatial terms, they appear to be on the way to becoming part
of the general U.S. black population."[38] If Denton and Massey
are correct, Puerto Ricans may eventually come to identify
themselves more in racial and less in ethnic terms, with darker
Puerto Ricans absorbed into the American black community
much as other Caribbean blacks, such as Jamaicans, have been
over time.

PUERTO RICAN POLITICS

If the social and economic status of Puerto Ricans is declining, what of their political power? Economic status per se is
not an absolute barrier to political participation—witness the
increasing political strength of urban blacks, who have elected
black mayors in five of the ten largest cities in the country in
recent years. Yet one of the chief impediments to Hispanic
political power is that the voting-age Hispanic population in
the United States consists of so many noncitizens. In Los Angeles, for example, less than half of all Hispanics are citizens.
Not only are many Hispanics recent immigrants, many of
them without legal status, but most of those who are eligible
to become citizens fail to do so.

Puerto Ricans suffer no such barriers to their participation
in the political process. They are eligible to vote in U.S. elections as soon as they satisfy state and local residency requirements that apply to all citizens. Yet Puerto Ricans, like
Mexican Americans, complain that they lack the political

power their numbers deserve. In order to wield that power, however, Puerto Ricans must vote, and few do. Only 33 percent of New York's Hispanic population was registered to vote in 1988, and only 28 percent voted, compared with nearly half of the blacks and 63.5 percent of the whites who were registered and with 41 percent of the blacks and 57 percent of the whites who voted.[39] At present, only one Puerto Rican is a voting member of Congress (the delegate from Puerto Rico does not have voting status), and only about 185 Puerto Ricans (out of a total of more than 4,000 Hispanic elected officials) hold other elected offices on the mainland, mostly in New York, New Jersey, Illinois, Pennsylvania, and Connecticut.[40]

Political participation in mainland politics is complicated by Puerto Ricans' relationship to the island. Puerto Ricans frequently move back and forth between the island and mainland over their lifetime. Candidates for office in Puerto Rico have traditionally campaigned in New York and other U.S. cities, even though only Puerto Ricans on the island actually vote in its elections. The division of migration of the Department of Labor and Human Resources of the Commonwealth of Puerto Rico also conducts massive voter registration drives for U.S. elections, including one in 1988 that registered more than 90,000 new voters. Puerto Rican leaders also note that political apathy is not a problem in elections on the island, where approximately 80 percent of those eligible actually vote.[41] Puerto Rico's status, however, cannot help having some effect on the attitudes of Puerto Ricans toward the political process, particularly since they retain a strong identification as Puerto Ricans first and Americans second, according to public opinion surveys.

Puerto Rico is neither fish nor fowl politically, neither a state nor an independent nation. Its inhabitants receive some federal benefits, including $6 billion in welfare assistance a year, pay no federal taxes, and are not allowed to vote in presidential elections. Puerto Rico has more autonomy than the U.S. Trust Territories, but its residents have even less power to influence U.S. politics than do residents of the District of Columbia (who may vote in presidential elections but whose congressional delegate may not cast votes in the House of Representatives except in committee). Moreover, Puerto Rico remains culturally distinct from the United States, with a population that is overwhelmingly Spanish speaking (although English is taught as a required subject in public schools and lessons in parochial and most private schools on the island are conducted in English).

Puerto Rico's future political status remains a controversial and unresolved issue. In 1990, the U.S. House of Representatives passed legislation allowing Puerto Ricans to vote on whether the island should become a state or an independent nation or remain a commonwealth, but after the Senate failed to act, the bill died at the end of the session. In early 1991, a senate committee killed a similar bill after several senators voiced concerns that a Puerto Rican state would become a burden on the federal government because most of the population would be eligible for welfare benefits. Further diminishing the prospects of Puerto Rican statehood, the Commonwealth legislature voted to make Spanish the island's sole official language, repealing a 1902 law that recognized both English and Spanish as official languages.

It is doubtful that, even if Puerto Rico achieved statehood, many New York Puerto Ricans would be enticed back to the island, since economic opportunity there is likely to continue to lag behind that on the mainland for some time to come; nor would it be likely to increase the flow of migrants from the island. Independence, on the other hand, might have a significant impact on Puerto Ricans. Questions of citizenship would have to be resolved. Puerto Ricans born in the United States would obviously retain U.S. citizenship. But those born on the island might have to choose between the two countries. A new, independent nation might balk at allowing significant portions of its population to hold dual citizenship, which raises the question of divided loyalties. It is conceivable that many Puerto Ricans on the island would choose to emigrate if asked to choose between an uncertain future in a new nation and the security of U.S. citizenship. In any event, it is unlikely that a change in Puerto Rico's status will do much to solve the problems that face Puerto Ricans in the United States.

WHERE DO PUERTO RICANS GO FROM HERE?

Many Puerto Ricans are making it in the United States. There is a thriving middle class of well-educated professionals, managers, and white-collar workers, whose individual earnings are among the highest of all Hispanic groups' and most of whom live in married-couple families.[42] These Puerto Ricans have done what other Hispanics and, indeed, most members of other ethnic groups have: they have moved up the economic ladder and into the social mainstream within one or two generations of their arrival in the United States.

Still, the prognosis for many other Puerto Ricans is not good. Each year brings evidence that more are slipping further into dependency and that Puerto Rican families are becoming increasingly dysfunctional. The illegitimacy rate for Puerto Rican babies inches up each year and is now over 50 percent. In 1960, 85 percent of all Puerto Rican males worked; three decades later, only 69 percent were in the labor force. Puerto Rican women swell the welfare rolls of New York City; and many are second-generation welfare recipients. Almost half of these women have never held a job. Puerto Ricans are being left behind not just by whites but by other Hispanics as well.

The crisis facing the Puerto Rican community is not simply

one of poverty and neglect. If anything, Puerto Ricans have been showered with too much government attention, but of the wrong kind. Citizenship, which should have enhanced Puerto Rican achievement, may actually have hindered it by conferring entitlements, such as welfare, with no concomitant obligations. The state has functioned too much like an anonymous *patrón*, dispensing welfare checks that allowed recipients to avoid the responsibilities of autonomous adults. The safety net became a web of dependency. While the life-style provided by the Department of Social Services is surely meager, it offers security. When the job market in New York became tight, only the most enterprising Puerto Ricans took the risk of leaving to search for work elsewhere. Those who did, and those who chose not to settle there in the first place, are doing better than Puerto Ricans in New York City. The fact that Puerto Ricans outside New York succeed proves there is nothing inevitable about Puerto Rican failure. Nor does the existence of prejudice and discrimination explain why so many Puerto Ricans fail when so many other Hispanics, including those from racially mixed backgrounds, are succeeding.

So long as significant numbers of young Puerto Rican men remain alienated from the work force, living by means of crime or charity, fathering children toward whom they feel no responsibility, the prospects of Puerto Ricans in the United States will dim. So long as so many Puerto Rican women allow the men who father their babies to avoid the duties of marriage and parenthood, they will deny their children the promise of a better life, which has been the patrimony of generations of poor immigrants' children. The solution to these problems will not be found in more government programs. Indeed, government has been an accomplice in enabling fathers to abandon their responsibility. Only the Puerto Rican community can save itself, but the healing cannot begin until the community recognizes that many of its deadliest wounds are self-inflicted.

CHAPTER 8

Toward a New Politics of Hispanic Assimilation

Assimilation has become a dirty word in American politics. It invokes images of people, cultures, and traditions forged into a colorless alloy in an indifferent melting pot. But, in fact, assimilation, as it has taken place in the United States, is a far more gentle process, by which people from outside the community gradually became part of the community itself. Descendants of the German, Irish, Italian, Polish, Greek, and other immigrants who came to the United States bear little resemblance to the descendants of the countrymen their forebears left behind. America changed its immigrant groups— and was changed by them. Some groups were accepted more reluctantly than others—the Chinese, for example—and some with great struggle. Blacks, whose ancestors were forced to come here, have only lately won their legal right to full participation in this society; and even then civil rights gains have not been sufficiently translated into economic gains. Until quite recently, however, there was no question but that each group desired admittance to the mainstream. No more. Now ethnic leaders demand that their groups remain separate, that their native culture and language be preserved intact, and that whatever accommodation takes place be on the part of the receiving society.

Hispanic leaders have been among the most demanding, insisting that Hispanic children be taught in Spanish; that Hispanic adults be allowed to cast ballots in their native language and that they have the right to vote in districts in which Hispanics make up the majority of voters; that their ethnicity entitle them to a certain percentage of jobs and college admissions; that immigrants from Latin America be granted many of these same benefits, even if they are in the country illegally. But while Hispanic leaders have been pressing these claims, the rank and file have been moving quietly and steadily into the American mainstream. Like the children and grandchildren of millions of ethnic immigrants before them, virtually all native-born Hispanics speak English—many speak only English. The great majority finish high school, and growing numbers attend college. Their earnings and occupational status have been rising along with their education. But evidence of the success of native-born Hispanics is drowned in the flood of new Latin immigrants—more than five million— who have come in the last two decades, hoping to climb the ladder as well. For all of these people, assimilation represents the opportunity to succeed in America. Whatever the sacrifices it entails—and there are some—most believe that the payoff is worth it. Yet the elites who create and influence public policy seem convinced that the process must be stopped or, where this has already occurred, reversed.

From 1820 to 1924 the United States successfully incorporated a population more ethnically diverse and varied than any other in the world. We could not have done so if today's politics of ethnicity had been the prevailing ethos. Once again, we are experiencing record immigration, principally from Latin America and Asia. The millions of Latin immigrants who are joining the already large native-born Hispanic population will severely strain our capacity to absorb them, unless we can revive a consensus for assimilation. But the new politics of Hispanic assimilation need not include the worst features of the Americanization era. Children should not be forced to sink or swim in classes in which they don't understand the language of instruction. The model of Anglo conformity would seem ridiculous today in a country in which 150 million persons are descended from people who did not come here from the British Isles. We should not be tempted to shut our doors because we fear the newcomers are too different from us ever to become truly "American." Nonetheless, Hispanics will be obliged to make some adjustments if they are to accomplish what other ethnic groups have.

LANGUAGE AND CULTURE

Most Hispanics accept the fact that the United States is an English-speaking country; they even embrace the idea. A *Houston Chronicle* poll in 1990 found that 87 percent of all Hispanics believed that it was their "duty to learn English" and that a majority believed English should be adopted as an official language.[1] Similar results have been obtained in polls taken in California, Colorado, and elsewhere. But Hispanics, especially more recent arrivals, also feel it is important to preserve their own language. Nearly half the Hispanics in the *Houston Chronicle* poll thought that people coming from other countries should preserve their language and teach it to their children. There is nothing inconsistent in these findings, nor are the sentiments expressed unique to Hispanics. Every immigrant group has struggled to retain its language, customs, traditions. Some groups have been more successful than others. A majority of Greek Americans, for example, still speak Greek in their homes at least occasionally.[2] The debate is not about whether Hispanics, or any other group, have the right to retain their native language but about whose responsibility it is to ensure that they do so.

The government should not be obliged to preserve any

group's distinctive language or culture. Public schools should
make sure that all children can speak, read, and write English
well. When teaching children from non-English-speaking
backgrounds, they should use methods that will achieve English proficiency quickly and should not allow political pressure to interfere with meeting the academic needs of students.
No children in an American school are helped by being held
back in their native language when they could be learning
the language that will enable them to get a decent job or
pursue higher education. More than twenty years of experience with native-language instruction fails to show that children in these programs learn English more quickly or perform
better academically than children in programs that empha-
size English acquisition.

If Hispanic parents want their children to be able to speak
Spanish and know about their distinctive culture, they must
take the responsibility to teach their children these things.
Government simply cannot—and should not—be charged
with this responsibility. Government bureaucracies given the
authority to create bicultural teaching materials homogenize
the myths, customs, and history of the Hispanic peoples of
this hemisphere, who, after all, are not a single group but
many groups. It is only in the United States that "Hispanics"
exist; a Cakchiquel Indian in Guatemala would find it remarkable that anyone could consider his culture to be the
same as a Spanish Argentinean's. The best way for Hispanics
to learn about their native culture is in their own communities. Chinese, Jewish, Greek, and other ethnic communities
have long established after-school and weekend programs to
teach language and culture to children from these groups.
Nothing stops Hispanic organizations from doing the same
things. And, indeed, many Hispanic community groups
around the country promote cultural programs. In Washington, D.C., groups from El Salvador, Guatemala, Colombia, and
elsewhere sponsor soccer teams, fiestas, parades throughout

the year, and a two-day celebration in a Latin neighborhood that draws crowds in the hundreds of thousands.[3] The Washington Spanish Festival is a lively, vibrant affair that makes the federal government's effort to enforce Hispanic Heritage Month in all of its agencies and departments each September seem pathetic by comparison. The sight and sound of mariachis strolling through the cavernous halls of the Department of Labor as indifferent federal workers try to work above the din is not only ridiculous; it will not do anything to preserve Mexican culture in the United States.

Hispanics should be interested not just in maintaining their own, distinctive culture but in helping Latin immigrants adjust to their American environment and culture as well. Too few Hispanic organizations promote English or civics classes, although the number has increased dramatically since the federal government began dispensing funds for such programs under the provisions of the Immigration Reform and Control Act, which gives amnesty to illegal aliens on the condition that they take English and civics classes.[4] But why shouldn't the Hispanic community itself take some responsibility to help new immigrants learn the language and history of their new country, even without government assistance? The settlement houses of the early century thrived without government funds. The project by the National Association of Latino Elected and Appointed Officials (NALEO) to encourage Latin immigrants to become U.S. citizens is the exception among Hispanic organizations; it should become the rule.

POLITICAL PARTICIPATION

The real barriers to Hispanic political power are apathy and alienage. Too few native-born Hispanics register and vote; too few Hispanic immigrants become citizens. The way to increase real political power is not to gerrymander districts to create safe seats for Hispanic elected officials or treat illegal aliens and other immigrants as if their status were unimportant to their political representation; yet those are precisely the tactics Hispanic organizations have urged lately. Ethnic politics is an old and honored tradition in the United States. No one should be surprised that Hispanics are playing the game now, but the rules have been changed significantly since the early century. One analyst has noted, "In the past, ethnic leaders were obliged to translate raw numbers into organizational muscle in the factories or at the polls. . . . In the affirmative-action state, Hispanic leaders do not require voters, or even protestors—only bodies."[5] This is not healthy, for Hispanics or the country.

Politics has traditionally been a great equalizer. One person's vote was as good as another's, regardless of whether the one was rich and the other poor. But politics requires that people participate. The great civil rights struggles of the 1960s were fought in large part to guarantee the right to vote. Hispanic leaders demand representation but do not insist that individual Hispanics participate in the process. The emphasis is always on rights, never on obligations. Hispanic voter organizations devote most of their efforts toward making the process easier—election law reform, postcard registration, election materials in Spanish—to little avail; voter turnout is still lower among Hispanics than among blacks or whites. Spanish posters urge Hispanics to vote because it will mean more and better jobs and social programs, but I've never seen one that mentions good citizenship. Hispanics (and others) need to be reminded that if they want the freedom and opportunity democracy offers, the least they can do is take the time to register and vote. These are the lessons with which earlier immigrants were imbued, and they bear reviving.

Ethnic politics was for many groups a stepping-stone into the mainstream. Irish, Italian, and Jewish politicians established political machines that drew their support from ethnic neighborhoods; and the machines, in turn, provided jobs and other forms of political patronage to those who helped elect them. But eventually, candidates from these ethnic groups went beyond ethnic politics. Governor Mario Cuomo (D) and Senator Alfonse D'Amato (R) are both Italian American politicians from New York, but they represent quite different political constituencies, neither of which is primarily ethnically based. Candidates for statewide office—at least successful ones—cannot afford to be seen merely as ethnic representatives. Ethnic politics may be useful at the local level, but if Hispanic candidates wish to gain major political offices, they will have to appeal beyond their ethnic base. Those Hispanics who have already been elected as governors and U.S. senators (eight, so far) have managed to do so.

EDUCATION

Education has been chiefly responsible for the remarkable advancements most immigrant groups have made in this society. European immigrants from the early century came at a time when the education levels of the entire population were rising rapidly, and they benefited even more than the population of native stock, because they started from a much lower base. More than one-quarter of the immigrants who came during the years from 1899 to 1910 could neither read nor write.[6] Yet the grandchildren of those immigrants today are indistinguishable from other Americans in educational attainment; about one-quarter have obtained college degrees. Second- and third-generation Hispanics, especially those who entered high school after 1960, have begun to close the education gap as well. But the proportion of those who go on to college is smaller among native-born Hispanics than among other Americans, and this percentage has remained relatively constant across generations, at about 10–13 percent for Mexican Americans. If Hispanics hope to repeat the successful experience of generations of previous immigrant groups, they must continue to increase their educational attainment, and they are not doing so fast enough. Italians, Jews, Greeks, and others took dramatic strides in this realm, with the biggest gains in college enrollment made after World War II.[7] Despite more than two decades of affirmative action programs and federal student aid, college graduation rates among native-born Hispanics, not to mention immigrants, remain significantly below those among non-Hispanics.

The government can do only so much in promoting higher education for Hispanics or any group. It is substantially easier today for a Hispanic student to go to college than it was even twenty or thirty years ago, yet the proportion of Mexican Americans who are graduating from college today is unchanged from what it was forty years ago. When the former secretary of education Lauro Cavazos, the first Hispanic ever to serve in the Cabinet, criticized Hispanic parents for the low educational attainment of their children, he was roundly attacked for blaming the victim. But Cavazos's point was that Hispanic parents must encourage their children's educational aspirations and that, too often, they don't. Those groups that have made the most spectacular socioeconomic gains—Jews and Chinese, for example—have done so because their families placed great emphasis on education.

Hispanics cannot have it both ways. If they want to earn as much as non-Hispanic whites, they have to invest the same number of years in schooling as these do. The earnings gap will not close until the education gap does. Native-born Hispanics are already enjoying earnings comparable to those of non-Hispanic whites, once educational differences are factored in. If they want to earn more, they must become better educated. But education requires sacrifices, especially for persons from lower-income families. Poverty, which was both more pervasive and severe earlier in this century, did not prevent Jews or Chinese from helping their children get a better education. These families were willing to forgo immediate pleasures, even necessities, in order to send their children to school. Hispanics must be willing to do the same—or else be satisfied with lower socioeconomic status. The status of second- and third-generation Hispanics will probably continue to rise even without big gains in college graduation; but the rise will be slow. Only a substantial commitment to the education of their children on the part of this generation of Hispanic parents will increase the speed with which Hispanics improve their social and economic status.

ENTITLEMENTS

The idea of personal sacrifice is an anomaly in this age of entitlements. The rhetoric is all about rights. And the rights being demanded go far beyond the right to equality under the law. Hispanics have been trained in the politics of affirmative action, believing that jobs, advancement, and even political power should be apportioned on the basis of ethnicity. But the rationale for treating all Hispanics like a permanently disadvantaged group is fast disappearing. What's more, there is no ground for giving preference in jobs or promotions to persons who have endured no history of discrimination in this country—namely, recent immigrants. Even within Hispanic groups, there are great differences between the historical discrimination faced by Mexican Americans and Puerto Ricans and that faced by, say, Cubans. Most Hispanic leaders, though, are willing to have everyone included in order to increase the population eligible for the programs and, therefore, the proportion of jobs and academic placements that can be claimed. But these alliances are beginning to fray at the edges. Recently, a group of Mexican American firemen in

San Francisco challenged the right of two Spanish Americans to participate in a department affirmative action program, claiming that the latter's European roots made them unlikely to have suffered discrimination comparable to that of other Hispanics. The group recommended establishing a panel of twelve Hispanics to certify who is and who is not Hispanic.[8] But that is hardly the answer.

Affirmative action politics treats race and ethnicity as if they were synonymous with disadvantage. The son of a Mexican American doctor or lawyer is treated as if he suffered the same disadvantage as the child of a Mexican farm worker; and both are given preference over poor, non-Hispanic whites in admission to most colleges or affirmative action employment programs. Most people think this is unfair, especially white ethnics whose own parents and grandparents also faced discrimination in this society but never became eligible for the entitlements of the civil rights era. It is inherently patronizing to assume that all Hispanics are deprived and grossly unjust to give those who aren't preference on the basis of disadvantages they don't experience. Whether stated or not, the essence of affirmative action is the belief that Hispanics— or any of the other eligible groups—are not capable of measuring up to the standards applied to whites. This is a pernicious idea.

Ultimately, entitlements based on their status as "victims" rob Hispanics of real power. The history of American ethnic groups is one of overcoming disadvantage, of competing with those who were already here and proving themselves as competent as any who came before. Their fight was always to be treated the same as other Americans, never to be treated as special, certainly not to turn the temporary disadvantages they suffered into the basis for permanent entitlement. Anyone who thinks this fight was easier in the early part of this century when it was waged by other ethnic groups does not know history. Hispanics have not always had an easy time of it in the United States. Even though discrimination against Mexican Americans and Puerto Ricans was not as severe as it was against blacks, acceptance has come only with struggle, and some prejudices still exist. Discrimination against Hispanics, or any other group, should be fought, and there are laws and a massive administrative apparatus to do so. But the way to eliminate such discrimination is not to classify all Hispanics as victims and treat them as if they could not succeed by their own efforts. Hispanics can and will prosper in the United States by following the example of the millions before them.

NOTES

Introduction

1. Raul Yzaguirre, speech at the Leadership Conference on Civil Rights Fortieth Annual Conference Dinner, May 8, 1990.
2. NALEO Education Fund, "First National Conference on Latino Children in Poverty," (Washington, D.C.: NALEO, 1987), 4.

Chapter 1: The Bilingual Battleground

1. Commission on Civil Rights, *Puerto Ricans in the United States: An Uncertain Future* (Washington, D.C.: GPO, 1976), 26–27. Net migration figures are from the Commonwealth of Puerto Rico Planning Board.
2. Commission on Civil Rights, *The Excluded Student: Educational Practices Affecting Mexican Americans in the Southwest* (Washington, D.C.: GPO, 1972).
3. Ibid.
4. James Crawford, *Bilingual Education: History, Politics, Theory, and Practice* (Trenton, N.J.: Crane, 1989), 28.
5. *Congressional Record*, 90th Cong., 1st sess., Dec. 1, 1967, 34703.
6. Diane Ravitch, *The Troubled Crusade: American Education, 1945–1980* (New York: Basic Books, 1983), 273.
7. The total figure was obtained in a Congressional Research Service memorandum to Representative Harris Falwell, "Es-

timated Funding Levels for Federal Programs that Assist in the Education of Limited English Proficient Individuals," Feb. 5, 1988. Title VII–funding figures are for fiscal year 1991.

8. Ravitch, *Troubled Crusade*, 272.

9. Senate, Select Committee on Equal Educational Opportunity, *Mexican American Education: Hearings*, 91st Cong., 2nd sess., 2424.

10. The OCR guideline read, "Where inability to speak and understand the English language excludes national origin-minority group children from the effective participation in the educational program offered by a school district, the district must take affirmative steps to rectify the language deficiency in order to open its instructional program to these students."

11. *Lau* v. *Nichols*, 414 U.S. 563 (1974).

12. Department of Health, Education, and Welfare, "Task Force Findings Specifying Remedies Available for Eliminating Past Educational Practices Ruled Unlawful under *Lau* v. *Nichols*," Washington, D.C., Summer 1975.

13. See Christine H. Rossell and J. Michael Ross, "The Social Science Evidence on Bilingual Education," *Journal of Law and Education* 15, no. 4 (Fall 1986): 150–68.

14. Crawford, *Bilingual Education*, 35.

15. Susan Gilbert Schneider, *Revolution, Reaction or Reform: The Bilingual Education Act of 1974* (New York: Las Americas, 1976), 48.

16. Ibid.

17. Cited in Crawford, *Bilingual Education*, 37.

18. "Evaluation of the Impact of ESEA Title VII Spanish/English Bilingual Education Program" (Palo Alto, Calif.: American Institutes for Research, 1978).

19. Senate, Select Committee on Equal Educational Opportunity, *Mexican American Education*, 2464–65.

20. Noel Epstein, *Language, Ethnicity, and the Schools: Policy Alternatives for Bilingual-Bicultural Education* (Washington, D.C.: Institute for Educational Leadership, 1977).

21. Harold Isaacs, "The One and the Many: What Are the Social and Political Implications of the New Ethnic Revival?" *American Educator* 2, no. 1 (Spring 1978): 13–14.

22. Ricardo L. Garcia, *Fostering a Pluralistic Society through Multi-Ethnic Education* (Bloomington, Ind.: Phi Delta Kappa Education Foundation, 1978).

23. Crawford, *Bilingual Education*, 40.

24. Ibid., 41.

25. Keith A. Baker and Adriana de Kanter, *Bilingual Education: A Reappraisal of Federal Policy* (Lexington, Mass.: Lexington Books, 1983).

26. Keith A. Baker and Adriana de Kanter, "Effectiveness of Bilingual Education: A Review of the Literature," Department of Education, Sept. 25, 1981, 14.

27. Ann C. Willig, "A Meta-Analysis of Selected Studies on the Effectiveness of Bilingual Education," *Review of Educational Research* 55, no. 3 (Fall 1985): 269–317. A 1991 U.S. Department of Education study which was hailed by bilingual education advocates as proving that bilingual education was as effective as English immersion in teaching English actually showed disappointing results for both programs. While substantial numbers of children in both the early-exit bilingual and the English immersion programs were able to pass English proficiency exams, only 26 percent of the immersion students and 17 percent of the bilingual students had been put into regular English-speaking classrooms after four years.

28. Kenji Hakuta, *Mirror of Language: The Debate on Bilingualism* (New York: Basic Books, 1986), 219.

29. Krashen claims his theories are borne out by experience in several bilingual education projects in California. However, the study of which he is coauthor and which purports to demonstrate the practical effectiveness of keeping Hispanic children in extended bilingual programs is highly flawed. Moreover, it was published by the California Association for Bilingual Education, hardly a disinterested party in the debate. See Stephen Krashen and Douglas Biber, *On Course: Bilingual Education in California* (Sacramento: California As-

sociation for Bilingual Education, 1988), and Keith Baker, "Bilingual Education: Partial or Total Failure?" (Paper presented at the 1990 Second Language Research Forum, University of Oregon, March 1, 1990).

30. Eduardo Hernandez-Chavez, "Language Maintenance, Bilingual Education, and Philosophies of Bilingualism in the United States," in James A. Alatis, ed., *International Dimension of Bilingual Education* (Washington, D.C.: Georgetown University Press, 1978), 546–47.

31. National Association for Bilingual Education Conference, San Antonio, Texas, April 4–7, 1984.

32. Nicolas Sanchez, "Bilingualism Creates More Problems Than Solutions," *Vista*, Nov. 7, 1987, 38.

33. Joan Baratz-Snowden et al., "Parent Preference Study," Educational Testing Service (1988), 54.

34. Desdemona Cardoza, "The Identification and Reclassification of LEP Students: A Study of Entry and Exit Classification Procedures," *NABE Journal* 11 (Fall 1986): 21–45.

35. "Language Proficiency Assessment Committee Procedure Handbook," Houston Independent School Districts Parent Survey of Home Language Grades k–8" (rev. 1982).

36. Ibid.

37. Ohio Department of Education, "Guidelines for the Establishment and Implementation of Entry and Exit Criteria for Bilingual Programs" (1983).

38. Division of Bilingual Education, University of the State of New York, New York State Education Department, Albany, "A Draft Regents Policy Paper and Proposed Action for Bilingual Education" (rev. Jan. 6, 1989).

39. Commonwealth of Massachusetts Board of Education, "Report No. 5 to the United States District Court, District of Massachusetts on Boston School Desegregation," vol. 2 (July 15, 1985): 74.

40. Ibid.

41. Ibid., 73.

42. Baratz-Snowden, "Parent Preference Study."

43. Rosalie Pedalino Porter, *Forked Tongue: The Politics of Bilingual Education* (New York: Basic Books, 1990), 21.
44. In *Teresa P. et al.* v. *Berkeley Unified School District, et al.*, filed in U.S. District Court, Northern District of California, the court rejected the plaintiffs' claim (Feb. 14, 1989).

Chapter 2: Hispanics and the Voting Rights Act

1. Abigail Thernstrom, *Whose Votes Count? Affirmative Action and Minority Voting Rights* (Cambridge: Harvard University Press, 1987), 2.
2. Joint Center for Political Studies, *Black Elected Officials: A National Roster* (Washington, D.C.: Joint Center for Political Studies, 1989).
3. Thernstrom, *Whose Votes Count?*, 15.
4. Ibid., 54.
5. *Allen* v. *State Board of Elections*, 393 U.S. at 569 (1969).
6. Thernstrom, *Whose Votes Count?* 51.
7. *Torres* v. *Sachs*, 381 F. Supp. 309 (S.D.N.Y. 1984).
8. Senate, Committee on the Judiciary, Subcommittee on Constitutional Rights, *Extension of the Voting Rights Act of 1965: Hearings*, 94th Cong., 1st sess. (Washington, D.C.: GPO, 1975), 544.
9. Staff memorandum entitled "Expansion of the Coverage of the Voting Rights Act," June 5, 1975, as cited in Thernstrom, *Whose Votes Count?* 55.
10. Senate, *Extension of the Voting Rights Act of 1965: Hearings*, 720.
11. Thernstrom, *Whose Votes Count?* 56.
12. Joint Memorial 17, passed by the New Mexico state senate by a vote of 35 to 0 and the state house of representatives by 39 to 2.
13. Cited in Thernstrom, *Whose Votes Count?* 56. McClesky and Merrill, "Mexican American Political Behavior," *Social Science Quarterly*, 53 (March 1973), 785–798.
14. Thernstrom, *Whose Votes Count?* 57.
15. Ibid., 56.

16. Testimony of Leonel Castillo, city comptroller, Houston, Texas, and Al Perez, of the Mexican American Legal Defense and Education Fund, in House of Representatives, *Hearings on the Extension of the Voting Rights Act* (Washington, D.C.: GPO, 1975), 880–883.

17. 42 U.S.C. 1973, sec. 2 (a).

18. House of Representatives, Subcommittee on Civil and Constitutional Rights, *Hearings on Extension of the Voting Rights Act of 1965* (Washington, D.C.: GPO, 1981), 889.

19. Ibid., 900.

20. Ibid. 900–902.

21. Mexican American Legal Defense and Education Fund, "MALDEF: The First Twenty Years, 1968–1988" (Los Angeles: MALDEF), 9.

22. In *Federation for American Immigration Reform (FAIR)* v. *Klutznick*, 486 F. Supp. 564 (D.D.C.), the Supreme Court in 1979 failed to grant certiorari, noting that FAIR failed to show that it had incurred a personal and concrete injury, which is required to establish standing.

23. Peter Skerry, "Keeping Immigrants in the Political Sweatshops," *Wall Street Journal*, Nov. 6, 1989.

24. Marita Hernandez, "Toward Equality: Exploring a World of Difference; Gloria Molina," *Los Angeles Times*, Feb. 13, 1989.

25. Interview with Carl Berry, of the Los Angeles Elections Division, Oct. 23, 1990.

26. Bureau of the Census, *Voting and Registration in the Election of November 1986*, Current Population Reports, ser. P-20, no. 414 (Washington, D.C.: GPO, 1987).

27. House, *Hearings on Extension of the Voting Rights Act of 1965* (1981), 900.

28. Douglas S. Massey and Nancy A. Denton, "Hypersegregation in U.S. Metropolitan Areas: Black and Hispanic Segregation along Five Dimensions," *Demography* 26, no. 3 (Aug. 1989): 383.

29. Richard Simon and Stephanie Chavez, "Upwardly Mobile Latinos Shift Their Political Views," *Los Angeles Times*, Dec. 26, 1987.

30. Rodolfo Acuña, "The Fight for the Spoils," *Los Angeles Times*, Aug. 12, 1990.

Chapter 3: The Power Brokers

1. National Association of Latino Elected and Appointed Officials, "National Roster of Hispanic Elected Officials" (1990). NALEO's figures do not indicate specific Hispanic subgroups; I made my estimate by identifying elected officials in states where Puerto Ricans and Cubans are the predominant Hispanic group.
2. Ralph Guzman, *The Political Socialization of the Mexican American People* (New York: Arno Press, 1976), 124.
3. Some estimates of the federal cost of resettling Cuban refugees go as high as a billion dollars over the decade. See Joan Moore and Harry Pachon, *Hispanics in the United States* (Englewood Cliffs, N.J.: Prentice-Hall, 1985), 193.
4. Edward D. Garza, "LULAC: League of United Latin American Citizens," Southwest Texas State Teachers College, 1951, 20.
5. Moore and Pachon, *Hispanics in the United States*, 185.
6. See Tony Castro, *Chicano Power* (New York: Saturday Review Press, 1974), 27.
7. Guzman, *Political Socialization*, 146.
8. Ibid., 144.
9. For example, see Richard Silva, "Writers Point Out Different Nationalities among Hispanics," *Albuquerque Tribune*, Jan. 4, 1990.
10. *The Official New Mexico Blue Book, 1987–1988*, Diamond Jubilee Commemorative Edition, 1912–1987. (Santa Fe: Rebecca Vigil-Giron, Secretary of State).
11. John H. Burma, *Spanish-Speaking Groups in the United States* (Durham: Duke University Press, 1954), 29.
12. Nancie L. Gonzalez, *The Spanish-Americans of New Mexico: A Heritage of Pride* (Albuquerque: University of New Mexico Press, 1967), 97.
13. Quoted in Castro, *Chicano Power*, 133.
14. Ibid., 100.

15. Moore and Pachon, *Hispanics in the United States*, 183.

16. Castro, *Chicano Power*, 39.

17. Ibid., 149. Other accounts, notably from the Ford Foundation program officer Siobhan O. Nicolau, contend that Gutierrez was provoked to make the statement by hostile questions from the press.

18. Siobhan O. Nicolau and Henry Santiestevan, *From the Eye of the Storm: Ernesto Galarza Latino History Series, Essay No. 1* (New York: Hispanic Policy Development Project, 1990), 16.

19. For an account of the Nixon "Chicano strategy" see Castro, *Chicano Power*, 198–215.

20. New York: Free Press, 1970.

21. Information provided by William Diaz, program officer, Human Rights and Governance, the Ford Foundation. The figures are accurate as of December 1990.

22. Information gathered from "Hispanics: Challenges and Opportunities" (Working Paper from the Ford Foundation, 1984).

23. Nicolau and Santiestevan, *From the Eye of the Storm*, 9.

24. Ibid., 5.

25. *Robert Alvarez* v. *Lemon Grove School District*, the earliest desegregation case involving Mexican American students, is poignantly recounted in *Familia: Migration and Adaptation in Baja and Alto California, 1800–1975*, by the plaintiff's son, Robert R. Alvarez, Jr. (Berkeley: University of California Press, 1987), 151–55.

26. Data cited from several separate studies of exogamous marriages in Moore and Pachon, *Hispanics in the United States*, 10.

27. Cited in Diane Ravitch, *Troubled Crusade: American Education, 1945–1980* (New York: Basic Books, 1983), 313.

28. A 1966 poll of Mexican Americans in San Antonio and Los Angeles found that under 1 percent of the respondents in either city were very familiar with or active in any of the contemporary Hispanic organizations. Only about 20 percent of the Mexican Americans in Los Angeles had heard of the G.I. Forum, and about 10 percent had heard of LULAC;

in San Antonio, nearly half of the respondents had never heard of the G.I. Forum and a quarter had never heard of LULAC. See Guzman, *Political Socialization*, 122–23.

Chapter 4: The Backlash

1. *Tampa Tribune*, Nov. 2, 1982.
2. A popular myth suggests that the Continental Congress considered making German the nation's official language and that the measure failed by one vote. A Library of Congress study of the issue found that neither the Continental Congress nor any session of Congress ever considered a proposal to make German the nation's official language. The myth probably grew from an incident in which a congressional vote was taken to make three thousand copies of federal laws available in German; the measure failed by one vote. See Heinz Kloss, *The American Bilingual Tradition* (Rowley, Mass.: Newbury House, 1977), 28.
3. Joshua Fishman et al., *Language Loyalty in the United States* (The Hague: Mouton, 1966).
4. Dade County (which includes Miami), Florida, also passed a countywide antibilingual referendum in 1980, which was largely a reaction to an earlier declaration by the Dade County Council proclaiming the county bilingual and bicultural. The 1980 declaration was modified in 1984 to allow emergency services and certain other functions to be carried out in Spanish. Four other states had passed official English laws before 1983.
5. The number of members is the number of persons who contribute to the organization annually.
6. The following states have statutes or constitutional amendments declaring English their official language: Alabama (1990); Arizona (1988); Arkansas (1987); California (1986); Colorado (1988); Florida (1988); Georgia (1986); Hawaii, which gives dual recognition to native Hawaiian (1978); Illinois (1969); Indiana (1984); Kentucky (1984); Mississippi (1987); Nebraska (1920); North Carolina (1987); North Da-

kota (1987); South Carolina (1987); Tennessee (1984); and Virginia (1950).

7. An Alabama referendum in 1990 received 89 percent of the popular vote.

8. While the genocide analogy might seem extreme, the concept or term *cultural genocide* is in fact a favorite among bilingual education enthusiasts, who warn that Hispanic children will become the victims of cultural genocide if they are not taught in their native language and about their native culture.

9. However, in 1986 Barbara Bush said in a speech at the National Press Club, "I foresee many problems if you don't make English the official language of the United States," adding in an interview afterward that she was "appalled" that the nation had no official language. She swiftly changed her position during the presidential election.

10. The First Amendment protects the right of store owners to display signs in whatever language they choose, as it does the right of employees to speak in whatever language they choose while not actually performing their jobs. The courts have usually upheld the right of employers to restrict employees' use of languages other than English while carrying out their duties, however. See *Jurado* v. *1150 Corporation*, 813 F. 2d 1406 Ninth Circuit (1987).

11. Memorandum to participants in Witan IV, dated Oct. 10, 1986.

12. "Only English Spoken Here," *Time*, Dec. 5, 1988, 29.

13. Testimony of Josue Gonzales, director of the Office of Bilingual Education, before the House Subcommittee on Education, Committee on Education and Labor, March 1974.

14. "Only English Spoken Here."

15. House Concurrent Memorial 2005, 1985.

16. Richard D. Lamm and Gary Imhoff, *The Immigration Time Bomb: The Fragmenting of America* (New York: Truman Talley Books, 1985), 77.

17. Edward Abbey, *One Life at a Time, Please* (New York: Henry Holt, 1988), 43.

18. Thomas Fleming, "The Real American Dilemma," *Chronicles*, March 1989, 9.

19. A federal district court in Arizona has in fact ruled that the First Amendment protects the right of government employees to use Spanish in the performance of their duties. That decision, which also ruled the Arizona official-English amendment unconstitutional, is now on appeal. In a similar case, the Ninth Circuit Court upheld that a radio station in California could fire a disc jockey who insisted on speaking Spanish on the air. See *Jurado* v. *1150 Corporation*, 813 F. 2d 1406 Ninth Circuit (1987).

20. Manuel del Valle, "Developing a Language-Based National Origin Discrimination Modality," *Journal of Hispanic Policy* 4 (1989–90): 72.

21. Strategy Research Corporation, "1989 U.S. Hispanic Market." A 1984 survey by Yankelovich, Skelly, and White showed 50 percent of the Hispanics identifying themselves as "Hispanic first/American second."

22. Nathan Glazer and Daniel P. Moynihan, *Beyond the Melting Pot: The Negroes, Puerto Ricans, Jews, Italians, and Irish of New York City*, 2d ed. (Cambridge: MIT Press, 1970), xxxiii.

23. Robert N. Hopkins, "Can the United States Assimilate the Wave of New Immigrants?" *Conservative Review* 1, no. 2 (April 1990).

24. Yankelovich, Skelly, and White, "Spanish USA 1984."

25. Oath of Allegiance, 22 Fed. Reg. 9824 (Dec. 6, 1957).

Chapter 5: An Emerging Middle Class

1. Raul Yzaguirre, speech at the Leadership Conference on Civil Rights Fortieth Anniversary Dinner, May 8, 1990.

2. See Alejandro Portes and Robert L. Bach, *Latin Journey: Cuban and Mexican Immigrants in the United States* (Berkeley: University of California Press, 1985). The earliest Cuban refugees included many businessmen, professionals, and skilled workers, but later immigrants were neither wealthy nor well educated.

3. L. H. Gann and Peter J. Duignan, *The Hispanics in the United States: A History* (Boulder, Colo.: Westview Press, 1986), 108.

4. Leo Grebler, Joan W. Moore, and Ralph C. Guzman, *The Mexican American People: The Nation's Second Largest Minority* (New York: Free Press, 1970), 187.

5. Bureau of the Census, *The Hispanic Population in the United States: March 1990*, Current Population Reports, ser. P-20, no. 449 (Washington, D.C.: GPO 1991).

6. National Council of La Raza, "The Decade of the Hispanic: An Economic Retrospective" (Washington, D.C.: National Council of La Raza, March 1990).

7. Jorge Chapa, "The Myth of Hispanic Progress: Trends in the Educational and Economic Attainment of Mexican Americans," *Harvard Journal of Hispanic Policy* 4 (1989–90): 17.

8. *Closing the Gap for U.S. Hispanic Youth: Report from the 1988 Aspen Institute Conference on Hispanic Americans and the Business Community* (Washington, D.C.: Hispanic Policy Development Project, 1988), 8.

9. Kenneth Prewitt, "Public Statistics and Democratic Politics," in William Alonso and Paul Starr, eds., *The Politics of Numbers* (New York: Russell Sage, 1987), 271.

10. Stephanie J. Ventura and Selma M. Taffel, "Childbearing Characteristics of U.S.- and Foreign-Born Hispanic Mothers," *Public Health Reports* 100, no. 6 (Nov.–Dec. 1985): 651.

11. For example, the sociologist Rafael Valdivieso has analyzed data from the U.S. Center for Education Statistics longitudinal study of young Americans, "High School and Beyond," and reports that Latina sophomores were more likely to rate having children as "very important" than their white non-Hispanic and black counterparts. See his "High School and Beyond: The Young Hispanic Woman," in Sara E. Rix, ed., *The American Woman, 1988–89* (New York: W. W. Norton, 1988).

12. In 1981 nearly 25 percent of all Hispanic mothers were under twenty years of age, according to the National Center for Health Statistics.

13. In 1986, 106 Hispanic women per 1,000 between the ages of

eighteen and forty-four gave birth to a child, compared with only 67 non-Hispanic women per 1,000 who did so. In other words, the fertility rate was almost 60 percent higher among Hispanic women than among non-Hispanic women. This difference is attributable almost exclusively to the number of Hispanic women who were having a second (or higher-order) child.

14. In 1987 only 36 percent of the Hispanic mothers with newborns were in the labor force, compared with 53 percent of the non-Hispanic mothers. See Bureau of the Census, *Fertility of American Women: June 1987* (Washington, D.C.: GPO, 1988).

15. See Leif Ingram Jensen, "Patterns of Immigration and Public Assistance Utilization, 1970–1980" (Madison: Center for Demography and Ecology, University of Wisconsin, 1986), 10.

16. Bureau of the Census, *The Hispanic Population . . . 1990.* The data do not present special classification for non-Hispanic whites.

17. Lawrence Mead, *Beyond Entitlement: The Social Obligations of Citizenship* (New York: Free Press, 1986), 71–72.

18. Lawrence Mead, *The New Dependency Politics: Nonworking Poverty in the U.S.* (forthcoming).

19. See Department of Labor, "Employment in Perspective: Minority Workers," Report 792, Aug. 1990.

20. These calculations were based on a sample of 1,889 Mexican-origin men, aged 25–65 from Current Population Survey data for 1986 and 1988. For more information write to the Manhattan Institute in New York.

21. Ibid.

22. Walter McManus, William Gould, and Finish Welch, "Earnings of Hispanic Men: The Role of English Language Proficiency," *Journal of Labor Economics* 1, no. 2 (April 1983): Also see Francisco L. Rivera-Batiz, "English Language Proficiency and the Economic Progress of Immigrants in the United States" (Paper presented at the Immigration Policy Group Conference, Department of Labor, Sept. 15–16, 1988).

23. Bureau of the Census, *Hispanic Population . . . 1990.* The per-

centage of Central/South Americans completing college dropped dramatically between 1989 and 1990, from 22 percent to 15 percent.

24. National Center for Education Statistics, *The Condition of Education: Postsecondary Education* (Washington, D.C.: GPO, 1990), 38.

25. Judith Cummings, "Hispanic People Gaining in New Jobs," *New York Times*, April 2, 1987.

26. Bureau of the Census, *Hispanic Population ... 1990*.

27. From Timothy Bates, "Hispanic-Owned Businesses" (Unpublished paper, July 1989, cited with permission of the author, a professor of economics at the New School for Social Research, Urban Policy Analysis Programs).

28. Bureau of the Census, *Hispanic Population ... 1990*.

29. In 1970 the poverty rate was about 29 percent for Mexican immigrants and 27 percent for Mexican Americans. In 1980 it decreased for both groups, to 26.5 percent for Mexican immigrants and to 21.6 percent for Mexican Americans. See Bean and Tienda, *The Hispanic Population of the United States* (New York: Russell Sage, 1987), 371.

30. Bureau of the Census, *Hispanic Population ... 1989*.

31. Douglas S. Massey and Nancy A. Denton, "Hypersegregation in U.S. Metropolitan Areas: Black and Hispanic Segregation along Five Dimensions," *Demography* 26, no. 3 (Aug. 1989): 373–91.

32. See Richard Alba, "Interethnic Marriage in the 1980 Census," in Stanley Lieberson and Mary C. Walters, eds., *From Many Strands: Ethnic and Racial Groups in Contemporary America* (New York: Russell Sage, 1988), 199.

33. National Council of La Raza, "Decade of the Hispanic."

34. National Council of La Raza, "Falling through the Cracks: Hispanic Underrepresentation in the Job Training and Partnership Act," (Washington, D.C.: National Council of La Raza, Feb. 1989).

35. A preliminary analysis of earnings of young Mexican American men aged sixteen to twenty-four from the 1986–88 Current Population Survey data suggests that they earned about

4 percent more than comparable non-Hispanic whites, though this may simply reflect a higher percentage of non-Hispanic white youths who are temporary workers and have not yet actually entered the labor force full-time.

36. A *San Francisco Examiner* study cited by John Bunzel in "Affirmative Action at Berkeley: How It Works," (*Public Interest*, no. 93 (Fall 1988): 111–29, shows that 66 percent of the non-Hispanic white students admitted to Berkeley, but only 41 percent of the Hispanic students graduate within five years.

37. Commission on Civil Rights, *The Economic Status of Americans of Southern and Eastern European Ancestry* (Washington, D.C.: GPO, 1986).

Chapter 6: The Immigrants

1. More than 400,000 additional Latin immigrants were granted legal resident-alien status under provisions of the Immigration Reform and Control Act (IRCA), which granted amnesty to illegal aliens who entered the United States prior to 1982. In all nearly 700,000 persons from Latin America were granted resident-alien status in 1989. The bulk of those admitted under IRCA were from Mexico, nearly 340,000 in 1989 alone. See Department of Justice, Immigration and Naturalization Service, *1989 Statistical Yearbook* (Washington, D.C.: GPO, 1990).

2. This number does not include persons granted legal status under IRCA. See note 1, above.

3. The number of apprehensions of illegals declined somewhat in 1987, after the Immigration Reform and Control Act's prohibitions against hiring illegal aliens went into effect, but has climbed once again to one million.

4. See Jeffrey Passell, "Undocumented Immigration," *Annals of the American Academy of Political and Social Science* (Sept. 1986): 181–200, and Frank D. Bean and Marta Tienda, *The Hispanic Population of the United States* (New York: Russell Sage, 1987) 118–21.

5. Immigration and Naturalization Service, *1989 Statistical*

Yearbook, 7. An additional seven thousand Cubans who arrived before 1989 adjusted their status in 1989.

6. Ibid.

7. The program was instituted in 1942 by an executive agreement between Mexico and the United States to provide
Mexican contract labor to American employers. Expanded
in 1951 by federal law, it created a steady stream of Mexican
agricultural workers to farms in California, Texas, and elsewhere. The program officially ended in 1960.

8. Alejandro Portes and Robert L. Bach, *Latin Journey: Cuban
and Mexican Immigrants in the United States* (Berkeley: University of California Press, 1985), 116.

9. Amara Bachu and Martin O'Connell, *Developing Current
Fertility Indicators for Foreign-Born Women from the Current Population Survey* (Washington, D.C.: Bureau of the Census, 1984).

10. George J. Borjas, *Friends or Strangers: The Impact of Immigrants
on the U.S. Economy* (New York: Basic Books, 1990), 108.

11. A number of studies confirm the link between English pro-
ficiency and higher earnings among immigrants. See espe-
cially Barry Chiswick and Paul Miller, "Language in the
Labor Market: The Immigrant Experience in Canada and the
United States" (Conference on Immigration, Language, and
Ethnic Issues, American Enterprise Institute, Washington,
D.C., 1991); and Franciso L. Rivera-Batiz, "English Language
Proficiency and the Economic Progress of Immigrants in the
United States" (Paper presented at the Immigration Policy
Group Conference, Department of Labor, Sept. 15–16 1988).

12. Portes and Bach, *Latin Journey,* 161.

13. Jerry Seper, "Arson Suspect, Local Scholar Are Two Sides of
Mariel Boatlift," *Washington Times,* March 28, 1990.

14. Alejandro Portes and Alex Stepick, "Unwelcome Immigrants," *American Sociological Review* 50 (Aug. 1985): 493–514.

15. Unfortunately, the sample size for the Current Population
Survey does not allow a breakdown by national origin group
within the category Central/South American. In 1990 some
2.8 million persons of Central or South American origin
were living in the United States. The large influx of immi-

grants from Central America because of guerrilla warfare and economic upheavals in the region during the 1980s suggests that this group increasingly comprises persons from Central America, however.

16. See Bean and Tienda, *Hispanic Population*, 329.

17. Thomas Sowell, *Ethnic America* (New York: Basic Books, 1981), 87–88.

18. Richard Alba, *Ethnic Identity: The Transformation of White America* (New Haven: Yale University Press, 1990), 6.

19. Richard A. Easterlin, "Immigration: Economic and Social Characteristics," in Stephan Thernstrom, ed., *Harvard Encyclopedia of American Ethnic Groups* (Cambridge: Harvard University Press, 1981), 476–86.

20. Sowell, *Ethnic America*, 23.

21. Alba, *Ethnic Identity*, 19.

22. Sowell, *Ethnic America*, 109.

23. Attempts early in this century to halt immigration from southern and eastern Europe included the passage of laws to prohibit those who were illiterate from immigrating, but these were vetoed by the president. The 1924 legislation accomplished a similar aim by tying the quota for admission from a given country to the proportion of persons from that country who resided in the United States in 1890, when there were fewer immigrants from eastern and southern Europe.

24. Richard D. Lamm and Gary Imhoff, *The Immigration Time Bomb: The Fragmenting of America* (New York: Truman Talley Books, 1985), 79.

25. See Borjas, *Friends or Strangers*, 13.

26. Roberto Suro, "1986 Amnesty Law Is Seen as Failing to Slow Alien Tide," *New York Times*, June 18, 1989. After declining somewhat after IRCA became effective, apprehensions of illegal aliens once again climbed to one million in 1989.

27. Immigration and Naturalization Service, *1989 Statistical Yearbook*, xi.

28. Department of Justice, Immigration and Naturalization Service, *1987 Statistical Yearbook* (Washington, D.C.: GPO, 1988).

29. Cited in Tracy Ann Goodis, *The Political Adaptation of His-*

panic Immigrants to the United States (Washington, D.C.: Urban Institute, Sept. 1988).

30. National Association of Latino Elected and Appointed Officials, "The National Latino Immigrant Survey," 1989.

31. Rodolfo O. de la Garza and Armando Trujillo, "Latinos and the Official English Debate in the United States: Language Is Not the Issue," University of Texas at Austin, April 1989.

32. *Plyler* v. *Doe*, 457 U.S. 202 (1982).

33. See Daniel Stein and Steven Zanowic, "Permanent Resident Aliens under Color of Law: The Opening Door to Alien Entitlement Eligibility," *Georgetown Immigration Law Journal*, 1 (Spring 1986): 231–67.

34. "Court Revives Challenge to 1982 Ballot Inquiry," *Los Angeles Times*, Aug. 27, 1986.

35. Jose Angel Gutierrez, speech at the National Council of La Raza annual meeting, Washington, D.C., July 17, 1990.

36. Comments made during a presentation at a conference on the Voting Rights Act at the Brookings Institution, Washington, D.C., Oct. 19, 1990.

37. See Kevin F. McCarthy and R. Burciaga-Valdez, *Current and Future Effects of Mexican Immigration in California* (Santa Monica, Calif.: Rand Corporation, 1986), 61; and Calvin Veltman, *The Future of the Spanish Language in the United States* (Washington, D.C.: Hispanic Policy Development Center, 1988).

38. Sowell, *Ethnic America*, 80–81.

39. Welfare rates, however, are lower among Mexican immigrants than among comparably poor native-born populations. Only about 5 percent of all Mexican immigrants, legal and illegal, received any welfare benefits in 1980, a much smaller percentage than that for other similarly poor persons. See McCarthy and Burciaga-Valdez, *Current and Future Effects of Mexican Immigration*, 49.

40. Borjas, *Friends or Strangers*, 155.

41. Barry Chiswick, "The Economic Progress of Immigrants: Some Apparently Universal Patterns," in Barry Chiswick, ed., *The Gateway: U.S. Immigration Issues and Policies* (Washington,

D.C.: American Enterprise Institute, 1982). See also Barry Chiswick, "Is the New Immigration Less Skilled Than the Old?" *Journal of Labor Economics* 4, no. 2 (April 1986): 168–91.

42. Borjas, *Friends or Strangers*, 118.
43. See NALEO, "National Latino Immigrant Survey," 25.
44. Michael J. White, *The Segregation and Residential Assimilation of Immigrants* (Washington, D.C.: Urban Institute, 1988).
45. Douglas S. Massey and Nancy A. Denton, "Suburbanization and Segregation in U.S. Metropolitan Areas," *American Journal of Sociology* 94 (Nov. 1988): 592–626.
46. Some studies suggest legal residents earn nearly 40 percent more than comparable illegal aliens. See D. Falasco and D. M. Heer, "Economic and Fertility Differences between Legal and Undocumented Migrant Mexican Families: Possible Effects of Immigration Policy Changes," *Social Science Quarterly* 65, no. 2 (1984): 495–504.
47. General Accounting Office, *Illegal Aliens: Influence of Illegal Workers on Wages and Working Conditions of Legal Workers* (Washington, D.C.: GPO, 1988).

Chapter 7: The Puerto Rican Exception

1. Joan Moore and Harry Pachon, *Hispanics in the United States* (Englewood Cliffs, N.J.: Prentice-Hall, 1985), 108.
2. Nathan Glazer and Daniel P. Moynihan, *Beyond the Melting Pot*, 2d ed. (Cambridge: MIT Press, 1986), 136.
3. Bureau of the Census, *The Hispanic Population in the United States: March 1988*, Current Population Reports, ser. P-20, no. 438 (Washington, D.C.: GPO, 1989). The 1990 report used elsewhere did not include a figure for median educational attainment for the Hispanic population.
4. Glazer and Moynihan, *Beyond the Melting Pot*, 118.
5. Joseph P. Fitzpatrick, *Puerto Rican Americans: The Meaning of Migration to the Mainland* (Englewood Cliffs, N.J.: Prentice-Hall, 1987), 75.
6. Ibid., 74.
7. Ibid.

8. L. H. Gann and Peter J. Duignan, *The Hispanics in the United States: A History* (Boulder, Colo.: Westview Press, 1986), 80.

9. "Hispanic ADC Recipients in New York City: Prospects for Employment and Self-Sufficiency," Office of Program Planning, Analysis and Development, New York State Department of Social Services, July 1990, 18.

10. Ibid.

11. Ibid., 49.

12. Ibid., 54.

13. Ibid., 80. A study of low-income Mexican American women found a similar antipathy toward placing children in child care centers. See *On My Own: Mexican American Women, Self-Sufficiency, and the Family Support Act* (Washington, D.C.: National Council of La Raza, 1990).

14. "Hispanic ADC Recipients," 65–66.

15. Fitzpatrick, *Puerto Rican Americans*, 102.

16. Bureau of the Census, *Hispanic Population ... March 1989*.

17. Lloyd H. Rogler and Rosemary Santana Cooney, *Puerto Rican Families in New York City: Intergenerational Processes* (Maplewood, N.J.: Waterfront Press, 1984). The study consisted of extensive interviews with one hundred Puerto Rican families consisting of two generations of parents and their adult, married children. Each of these families consisted of an intact married couple in which both partners were Puerto Rican and the couple's son or daughter, also married to a Puerto Rican spouse at the time of the study. Most of the parent-generation couples were in their fifties; most of the child-generation couples in the study were in their thirties and had been married about ten years.

18. Bureau of the Census, *Persons of Spanish Origin in the United States: March 1975*, Current Population Reports, ser. P-20, no. 290 (Washington, D.C.: GPO, 1976).

19. Rogler and Cooney, *Puerto Rican Families*, 127.

20. Bureau of the Census, *Persons of Spanish Origin ... March 1975*.

21. June O'Neill et al., *The Economic Progress of Black Men* (Washington, D.C.: Commission on Civil Rights, 1986), 180–81.

22. Rogler and Cooney, *Puerto Rican Families*, 155.

23. Bureau of the Census, *Money Income and Poverty Status in the United States: 1989*, Current Population Reports, ser. P-60, no. 168 (Washington, D.C.: GPO, 1990).

24. The earnings of Puerto Rican men, however, were probably less than those of Mexican American men, although published data do not provide sufficient data for us to make such a comparison, and I did not examine earnings for Puerto Rican men in my own analysis of unpublished data. It may contribute to higher earnings among Puerto Ricans that a large percentage of them live in high-wage states, such as New York and New Jersey.

25. Bureau of the Census, *Hispanic Population ... March 1989*. Puerto Ricans are more likely to live in high-wage states, which may partially explain the higher ratio of their earnings.

26. Rodriguez, *Puerto Ricans*, 46.

27. Fitzpatrick, *Puerto Rican Americans*, 66–67.

28. Julie Teresa Quiroz, *Twenty-two Hispanic Leaders Discuss Poverty* (Washington, D.C.: National Council of La Raza, 1990), 18–24.

29. Ibid., 22.

30. Some 71.5 percent of young Puerto Ricans have completed four years of high school or more, compared with about 79 percent of Mexican Americans, 84 percent of Cubans, and 89 percent of non-Hispanics. See Bureau of the Census, *Hispanic Population ... March 1990*, and table 2 in text.

31. *Imprisoned Generation: Young Men under Criminal Justice Custody in New York State* (New York: New York State Coalition for Criminal Justice, 1990).

32. Anna Stern, "Immigrants and Refugees: Some Considerations for Training the Workforce in the Future" (Paper prepared for the National Commission on Employment Policy, July 1990).

33. "Hispanic ADC Recipients in New York," 49.

34. Stern, "Immigrants and Refugees," 7.

35. Fitzpatrick, *Puerto Rican Americans*, 35.

36. More than half of the Hispanics who live in New York City are not Puerto Rican, and 68 percent of the Hispanic residents of Queens are not Puerto Ricans. See Governor's Advisory Committee for Hispanic Affairs, "New York State Hispanics: A Challenging Minority."

37. Rodriguez, *Puerto Ricans*, 92.

38. Nancy A. Denton and Douglas S. Massey, "Racial Identity among Caribbean Hispanics: The Effect of Double Minority Status on Residential Segregation" (Paper prepared for the Population Research Center and the University of Chicago, Aug. 1988), 26.

39. Bureau of the Census, *Voting and Registration in the Election of November 1988*, Current Population Reports, ser. P-20, no. 435. Voting statistics published by the Census Bureau do not distinguish separate Hispanic ethnic groups, so these figures include all Hispanics, not just Puerto Ricans. This practice tends to overestimate the number of eligible voters since it relies on voting age and includes many other Hispanics who are not citizens.

40. National Association of Latino Elected and Appointed Officials, "National Roster of Hispanic Elected Officials" (1990).

41. Nydia M. Velazquez, secretary of the Department of Puerto Rican Community Affairs in the United States, quoted in Doreen Carvajal and Denise-Marie Santiago, "Puerto Ricans: Adrift in Two Worlds," *Philadelphia Inquirer*, May 6–7, 1990.

42. Although the proportion of female-headed households is nearly 40 percent among Puerto Ricans, more than half of all Puerto Rican families still consist of a married couple. Bureau of the Census, *Hispanic Population ... March 1990*.

Chapter 8: Toward a New Politics of Hispanic Assimilation

1. Jo Ann Zuniga, "87% in Poll See Duty to Learn English," *Houston Chronicle*, July 12, 1990.

2. Commission on Civil Rights, *The Economic Status of Americans of Southern and Eastern European Ancestry* (Washington, D.C.: GPO, 1986), 45.

3. In May 1991, a riot broke out in a Latino neighborhood in Washington, D.C., where many new immigrants live (many of them illegal aliens). Both the local and national media described the two nights of arson and looting in political terms, as an expression of the alienation of the Hispanic community. In fact, fewer than half of the people arrested during the incident were Hispanic; most were young black males from a nearby neighborhood. There were few injuries and no deaths, and much criticism was directed at the police by local residents for standing by while young men looted stores, many of which were owned by Latinos. The Washington, D.C., metropolitan area is home to nearly a quarter of a million Hispanics, more than 80 percent of whom live in the suburbs of the city, far from the neighborhood where this incident occurred. Nonetheless, national Hispanic leaders, including members of the Hispanic Congressional delegation, flocked to the scene of the violence to portray as typical of the area's Latino population the problems which occurred in the few blocks of this urban settlement of recent immigrants.

4. For fiscal year 1989 the federal government distributed nearly $200 million in grants to state and local governments to assist in providing English and civics classes for adults and other services for those eligible for amnesty.

5. Peter Skerry, "Keeping Immigrants in the Political Sweatshops," *Wall Street Journal*, Nov. 6, 1989.

6. Richard A. Easterlin, "Immigration: Economic and Social Characteristics," in Stephan Thernstrom, ed., *Harvard Encyclopedia of American Ethnic Groups* (Cambridge: Harvard University Press, 1981), 478.

7. See Richard Alba, *Ethnic Identity: The Transformation of White America* (New Haven: Yale University Press, 1990), 7. Both men and women born after 1930 showed large gains, although the gains were higher for men, probably reflecting the increase in college attendance by veterans under the G.I. Bill.

8. "Spanish Progeny Are Not Hispanic, S.F. Group Insists," *San Diego Union*, Nov. 24, 1990. Ironically, both Spanish American firemen would have been promoted in the department even without benefit of affirmative action; they received the third- and sixth-highest scores on exams administered to sixty-eight persons for twenty promotion slots.

INDEX